First Time in London

Library of
Davidson College

FIRST TIME IN LONDON

by

Jack W. Meiland

CHARLES SCRIBNER'S SONS
NEW YORK

For Rosalie

Copyright © 1979 Jack W. Meiland

Library of Congress Cataloging in Publication Data

Meiland, Jack W.
    First time in London.

    Includes index.
    1. London—Description—1951-   —Guide-books.
I. Title.
DA679.M425   914.21'04'857   78-21547
ISBN 0-684-16045-5

THIS BOOK PUBLISHED SIMULTANEOUSLY IN THE
UNITED STATES OF AMERICA AND IN CANADA—
COPYRIGHT UNDER THE BERNE CONVENTION

ALL RIGHTS RESERVED. NO PART OF THIS BOOK
MAY BE REPRODUCED IN ANY FORM WITHOUT THE
PERMISSION OF CHARLES SCRIBNER'S SONS

1 3 5 7 9 11 13 15 17 19 V/C 20 18 16 14 12 10 8 6 4 2

PRINTED IN THE UNITED STATES OF AMERICA

Contents

INTRODUCTION vii
Why This Book? • How This Book Helps You • Why Go to London? • The Best Way to See London

PART ONE: GENERAL INFORMATION AND ADVICE 1
Getting There • Taxis • The Tube • Buses • Money and Credit Cards • How to Use an English Coin Phone • Weather and Dress • Medical and Dental Care • Finding a Place to Stay • Safety • Names for Parts of London • Radio and Television • Floors • Shopping • 35mm Photography • Architecture • Bookstores • Street Numbering • Pubs • Theater, Concerts, and Opera • Our Guide to Guide Books and Guides

PART TWO: SUGGESTED SCHEDULES 35
First Week Schedule • Second Week Schedule • Third Week Schedule

PART THREE: MAJOR PLACES OF INTEREST 39
The British Museum • The Houses of Parliament • Westminster Abbey • The Changing of the Guard at Buckingham Palace • The Tower of London • The National Gallery • The Victoria and Albert Museum • St. Paul's Cathedral • Hampton Court • Greenwich • Kew Gardens • Windsor Castle

CONTENTS

PART FOUR: LESS FREQUENTED PLACES OF EXCEPTIONAL INTEREST 55

The Banqueting House • St. Martin's-in-the-Fields • The National Portrait Gallery • Lancaster House • The Queen's Gallery and the Royal Mews • St. James's Park at Night • Pickering Place • Queen Anne's Gate • The Tate Gallery • Kensington Palace • The York Water Gate • The Hungerford Arches • St. Paul's, Covent Garden • Goodwin's Court • Home House • The Wallace Collection • Fitzroy Square • Bedford Square • Charles Dickens's House • The Percival David Collection • The Courtauld Institute Galleries • Sir John Soane's Museum • Dr. Samuel Johnson's House • Prince Henry's Room • St. Bartholomew the Great • The Museum of London • Leadenhall Market • Southwark Cathedral • The George Inn • Keats House and Fenton House • Kenwood House • Osterley House and Park • Hatfield House

PART FIVE: TWENTY ORIGINAL WALKS 79

A Roman London Walk • Kensington Gardens and the Museums • Southwark and London Bridge • Bloomsbury Squares and Museums • St. Paul's Cathedral and the Museum of London • Across the Thames from the South Bank Arts Centre • Around Regent's Park • Regent's Park to the Mall • Mayfair • St. James's Park, Queen Anne's Gate, and Banqueting House • The Strand, St. Martin's Lane, and Covent Garden • Legal London • A City Church Walk • Squares of the West End • Marylebone • Hanover Square to Piccadilly • Between Portland Place and Bloomsbury • Soho • Knightsbridge and South Kensington • Three Walks for a Nice Sunday Afternoon (1) Queen Mary's Gardens, Regent's Park (2) The Victoria Embankment (3) Hyde Park

IMPORTANT PHONE NUMBERS 100

INDEX 101

INTRODUCTION

1. WHY THIS BOOK?

Every day people arrive in London with little idea of what to do and see. Many leave after visiting only a few of the most famous places of interest and without getting to know London at all. Those who take tours spend their time riding the tour bus from one major "sight" to another, at the end of which they have a collection of "sights" and no feel for the city. Those who shun tours often spend the first few days of their precious time in London finding out what to see and how to see it, with the result that they waste much time; and time can slip away so rapidly on vacation.

This book is for the person going to London for the first time and who has only one, two, or three weeks to spend there. It is for the independent traveler who wants to arrange his or her own schedule and needs suggestions and advice on what is worthwhile and how to fit things together. Our aim is to put you in a position to spend your time most fruitfully the minute you arrive.

But aren't there already plenty of guide books to London? Yes, there are; some of them are excellent at the kind of thing they try to do, and we tell you about them later. But these books do not give you the explicit, detailed help you need to plan your time well. We try to give you down-to-earth, practical information directed at making your stay in London fuller and more enjoyable.

2. HOW THIS BOOK HELPS YOU

We begin with information and tips on how to get around in the city, finances, accommodations, guides and guide books, radio and TV, and other topics to get you oriented quickly to the general features of the London scene.

In later sections, we give you suggested schedules for visiting places of interest; brief descriptions of both major places and much less crowded but exceptionally interesting places along with advice about seeing them and full details about how to get there; and finally twenty original walks through various parts of the city to help you become better acquainted with London. By following our schedules for the first week or two, you will be spending your time well. After that, you will have your own ideas about what to see, based on our brief descriptions.

3. WHY GO TO LONDON?

People go to London for many reasons—for wonderful theater, for the shopping, for the active musical life. But the best reason of all is to experience and enjoy what is perhaps the greatest and most civilized city in the world today.

Big cities are receiving a bad press these days. They are said to be noisy, dirty, overcrowded, dangerous, and inhuman—and this is true of many cities. But a great city can be alive and exciting in a unique and priceless way. And London affords the visitor the opportunity to be part of a great city. The visitor who sees only Oxford Street, the Tower, and Westminster Abbey misses this opportunity completely. This kind of opportunity is increasingly less available in America.

But people who find New York City harsh will find London humane. Those who find Chicago dangerous will find London safe. Everyone will find London to be a cosmopolitan city with a definite character of its own: urbane, lively, hospitable, relaxed, cultured, and with a strong sense of and love for its past.

You should have no compunctions or qualms about being a visitor in London. If you are polite and courteous, Londoners will be glad that you have come. They are very proud of their city and of the fact that it attracts so many people from all over the world. Tourism is now England's third largest industry, and your money and that of other visitors helps to preserve those priceless cultural assets that make London what it is.

4. THE BEST WAY TO SEE LONDON

The advice of William Gladstone, the Victorian prime minister—that the best way to see London is from the top of a bus—no longer applies. On today's fast, enclosed buses you are insulated from the city, and buildings and people flash by before you have had a good look at them. Moreover, as Kingman Brewster, the American ambassador to England and a self-confessed London addict, recently said, "London is a wonderful town to walk in."

Because walking in London is so enjoyable and instructive, this book emphasizes walks. This is fine for those who enjoy walking, but what about those who don't enjoy it? They can do quite well by a judicious use of taxis, since taxis in Central London are numerous, fast, and relatively inexpensive; leave the taxi before you get to your destination and walk a few blocks to get the "feel" of the neighborhood.

Part One

GENERAL INFORMATION AND ADVICE

1. GETTING THERE

If you possibly can, take Laker Airways, either on a charter arranged through your travel agent or by Skytrain from New York. The reason is that Freddy Laker is single-handedly responsible for the recent drastic reduction in transatlantic air fares. He fought the big companies and won. Then the scheduled airlines—TWA, British Airways, and others—lowered their fares in response to Laker's competition. Many observers of the air-travel scene—including the Justice Department—believe that if Laker is forced to abandon Skytrain, the other airlines will raise their rates back to the old high levels. So it is in our interests as travelers to fly Laker whenever possible and help keep air fares down.

Laker flies into London's Gatwick Airport. The other airlines land at Heathrow. It is as easy to get into Central London from Gatwick as it is from Heathrow. Trains leave Gatwick very frequently and let you off at Victoria Rail Station, which has swarms of taxis and is also adjacent to Victoria subway station. A subway line to Heathrow has recently opened, making the trip from that airport to Central London simple and fast.

Most transatlantic flights leave America in the early evening and arrive in England fairly early the next morning. Since the flight attendants continually bother you with offers of food, drinks, and movies, it is difficult to sleep during the flight and you arrive somewhat fatigued the next morning. Because of this fatigue, you may wish to rest the day you arrive. However, we strongly advise you not to sleep for a long period that day but to attempt to get on to your new schedule right away by waiting until that evening to go to sleep. Otherwise, your vacation may be out of kilter for several days. On that first day, you may wish to see only Westminster Abbey which is not taxing to visit and which is very near a subway station.

2. TAXIS

How to hail a taxi: stand at the curb; when you spot a taxi with its roof light on (showing that it is not engaged), raise your arm straight up and wave it a bit. The light is hard to see in the daytime; so when in doubt, raise your arm anyway. Tell the driver through the front window where you want to go (he will be on the other side of the vehicle), and when he agrees, climb in. Upon arrival, he will tell you what the fare is, and you should add 15 to 20 percent as a tip. (The tip is easily calculated since British currency is on the decimal system now. See Money and Credit Cards section below.)

There are 11,500 taxis in London. Consequently they are easy to find, at least in Central London—except during morning and evening rush hours and during heavy rain.

Taxis can be obtained by telephone. Here are some numbers to try: 286-4848, 272-3030, 286-6010. Taking a radio taxi this way is somewhat more expensive than taking a taxi on the street.

3. THE TUBE

The tube is the London Underground, or subway system. Some guide books will tell you to avoid the tube because you cannot see anything of the city while you travel; they advise taking the bus instead. We disagree with this. If you are a visitor with limited time, you can save great amounts of time by taking the tube rather than the bus, which is much slower. Buses give you only fleeting glimpses of the city anyway. Moreover, you might wait half an hour for a bus and then find (especially during rush hour) that the bus which arrives is too crowded to board. (Bus conductors are very fierce in making sure that only the permitted number do board.)

When you buy your ticket at the tube station, ask for a free tube diagram. All transfers on the tube from one line to another are free. Tickets are green or yellow. Green tickets are shown to gate attendants, while yellow tickets are slipped into the lower (nearer) slot of a turnstile and retrieved from the upper slot as you pass through. In either case you must give up your ticket to a gate attendant at the end of your journey, so hold on to it during the trip. You can buy round-trip tickets to save the nuisance of buying another ticket on the way home, but round-trip tickets do not save you money except on long trips. Ask for a round-trip ticket by using the word "return"; for example, saying "two return to Trafalgar Square" will give you two round-trip tickets between your present station and Trafalgar Square. Buying a ticket is called "booking a ticket," not only on London Transport but also elsewhere, such as in theaters. London Transport offers reduced-rate passes, such as the Central London Tube Rover and the Red Bus Rover.

You can recognize a tube station by the following symbol: a red circle bisected horizontally by a red bar. Once you have bought your ticket and have gone to the platform by stairs, elevator, or escalator, you should check the *front* of each train to make sure that the one you take is going on the branch line that you want and as far on that branch as you want to go. Most trains stop at all stations on their branch. Inside each car are placards with a diagram of the line on which you are traveling, and you can keep track of where you are by referring to them. The tube diagram for the complete system is also found on the walls of each tube station platform.

Each of the fifteen stations of British Rail in Central London has a tube station in it or very near it. The tube station has the same name as the rail station, with three exceptions: for Charing Cross the tube is Embankment; for Holborn Viaduct the tube is St. Paul's; for Fenchurch Street the tube is Tower Hill.

Children under the age of three travel free. Those between the ages of three and thirteen pay reduced fares.

You can get London Transport publications and information at the Travel Inquiry Office at the following tube stations: St. James's Park, Euston, King's Cross, Oxford Circus, Victoria, and Piccadilly Circus. For questions about how to get from one place to another, you may call 222-1234.

Each subway train has one smoking car in every group of three or four cars. You can find "no smoking" cars by looking at the London Transport red circle symbol on the car window; "No Smoking" will be printed across the symbol.

On escalators, stand on the right so that the people walking up or down can pass. One of the commonest complaints that Londoners have about visitors is that many of them forget to stand on the right.

Finally, remember that the tube stops running around midnight; after midnight, take a taxi.

4. BUSES

First, obtain a copy of the leaflet "London Transport Official Tourist Information" at any Travel Inquiry Office (see

GENERAL INFORMATION AND ADVICE

previous section for locations). Some tube ticket offices will also have these leaflets. These leaflets have a useful map of Central London on one side with bus routes clearly marked. The other side has a tube diagram and useful travel information.

Buses in Central London are of the red double-decker variety with the top deck enclosed. Catch a bus by first locating the proper bus stop. If its sign has a black bar across the center of the red circle, it is a compulsory stop, which means that all buses on the route will stop automatically there. If the sign instead has the word "request" on it, you must stop the bus yourself by raising your arm. If other people are also waiting, then line up behind them. (This is called "queueing," and all Londoners do it. The other great Londoner complaint is about visitors who refuse to queue.) Take your seat on either deck, and eventually the conductor will come to you, ask you where you are going, and collect the fare. He will then print you a receipt on the spot. Keep this receipt until you get off because an inspector might ask to check it at any time; if you do not have the receipt, you will have to pay again. Children under five travel free on buses, and children five through fifteen pay reduced fares.

There is smoking only on the upper decks of double-decker buses and none at all on single-deckers. Single-deckers are now found mainly in the suburbs; they have no conductor and you pay the driver as you enter at the front. The driver or conductor will tell you when to get off if you ask him to do so.

At each bus stop there are charts of the routes that stop there. You must, of course, make sure that you are standing on the proper side of the street for the direction in which you wish to go.

Green Line buses travel between Central London and points on the outskirts of the city.

Some buses (particularly those without conductors) display a sign saying "Exact fare only." This does not mean that they will not give some change but only that they will not change pound notes.

There are *no* free transfers on the bus system. You have to pay all over again every time you get on another bus.

5. MONEY AND CREDIT CARDS

The best way to handle your money is to convert it all to American traveler's checks before you leave and then change them to pounds sterling as the need arises. There is no point in establishing a checking account in England for a short period of time—and it is usually impossible, anyway, since it takes several weeks to do this. Do not take your money in the form of money orders, cashier's checks, or certified checks; these are very difficult to cash in London, and some visitors have found them impossible to cash, leaving them in a difficult financial situation. Convert your traveler's checks into cash at a bank, since banks have the best exchange rates and there are branches of the four clearinghouse banks throughout Central London. Some branches post the daily exchange rate in their street windows. Banking hours are 9:30 A.M. to 3:30 P.M., Monday through Friday. On Friday, make sure that you have enough cash to get you through the weekend.

The only type of crime that you need to be concerned about in London is having your pocket picked. So don't carry large amounts of cash. Don't carry your passport around with you (except when going to cash a traveler's check). And do keep the numbers of your uncashed traveler's checks in a safe place in your lodgings.

Some years ago the English switched from their old monetary system of pounds, shillings, and pence to a decimal system with the following notes and coins: one-pound, five-pound, ten-pound, and twenty-pound notes; coins of fifty pence, ten pence, five pence, two pence, one pence, and one-half pence. Each pound sterling is worth one hundred pence. The fifty-pence coin and the ten-pence coin are both silver-colored and about the same size, but the fifty-pence coin is seven-sided while the ten-pence coin is round. Coins of the old system are still circulating to some extent, but the only ones that you are likely to come across are the two-shilling piece and the one-shilling piece. Here is how to use these old coins: the two-shilling piece is exactly the same size, shape, and color as the ten-pence piece and is worth exactly ten pence; the one-shilling piece is the same size, shape, and color as the five-pence piece and is worth five pence; so these two old coins can be used just as if they were these new coins. Prices are given in pounds (£) and pence (p). Thus, a man's shirt might cost £4.95 (said "four pounds ninety-five"). To pay this, you might use four one-pound notes, one fifty-pence coin, four ten-pence coins, and one five-pence coin. £4.95 is exactly the same as 495 pence (because each pound is worth one hundred pence), so the price could have been written "495p" instead. People usually *say* "p" rather than "pence." The exchange rate with American dollars has recently hovered in the area of £1 = $1.80 to $2.00. With rates in this range, you can easily figure out the price of English goods in American dollars by simply doubling the English price and then taking off a small amount. Thus, a £5 shirt would cost about $9.

In general, English prices on clothing and other goods are at about the level of American prices for the same sort of merchandise; one shouldn't go to England expecting to find great bargains as a normal matter. Of course, bargains are available, just as they are anywhere, but you have to shop around to find them. Many French, German, Dutch, and other Europeans do come to London in droves to shop, because London prices on goods have been substantially below continental prices; but they are not substantially below

American prices. However, if you are going on to France or Germany, be sure to buy everything you need in London rather than wait until you get to the continent.

It is useful to have one or two credit cards to supplement your cash. The American Express credit card issued in America is, of course, acceptable everywhere in London that takes American Express at all. The Visa (BankAmericard) card is issued in England by Barclays Bank, and many places have Visa stickers in their windows. But *not* every shop in England with a Visa sign will take a Visa card *issued in America;* you will have to ask each time you want to use the card. If you think that you might want to call America while in England, obtain a telephone credit card from your phone company before you leave. This allows you to charge calls to your home phone and makes the placing of transatlantic calls much easier. (Don't forget the six-to-eight-hour time difference when you call.)

A worthwhile precaution is to obtain an American Express Courtesy Card from the American bank where you have a checking account before you leave. You do *not* have to have an American Express credit card to obtain a courtesy card, and your bank will supply this courtesy card free of charge. This courtesy card allows you to buy American Express traveler's checks in London up to $250 by merely writing a check on your American bank. If you are married, your husband or wife can also obtain a separate courtesy card, thus giving the two of you a total of $500 in reserve funds in case of need. At the time you use this card to get your traveler's checks, you must turn in the card; so the card can be used only once, and it is good for only six months from the time it is issued. To use this card in London, go to the American Express office at 6 Haymarket (near Pall Mall; use Piccadilly Circus or Trafalgar Square tube).

6. HOW TO USE AN ENGLISH COIN PHONE

English coin phones differ from American coin phones in this way: with an American coin phone, you pay first and then dial your number, getting your money back if no one answers; with an English coin phone, you pay only after someone has answered. English coin phones have slots for 2p and 10p coins, so equip yourself with a supply of these before dialing. If the number you are calling is in London and you are in London, do *not* dial the London area code "01." After dialing, you will hear the phone at the other end ring—all London phones give two short rings, a pause, and then two short rings again. When your party answers, their voice will be cut off and replaced by a high beeping sound. This is a signal that the coin slot is now unlocked and that you should push in a 2p or a 10p coin. Once the coin drops, your party will come back on the line to say "hello" again, and you can carry on with your conversation. The coin that you pushed in buys you a certain amount of time to talk. When that time is up, the high beeping sound will begin again, and you can push in another coin to continue your conversation before you are cut off. There are two ways to avoid being interrupted regularly by that beeping sound: (1) push in more coins while you are talking with your party; the coin slots stay unlocked while the conversation is going on, and you can push in additional coins at any time; (2) if your party has a non-coin phone, ask them to call you back at your coin phone so that no one has to push in any coins; Londoners will often suggest calling you back anyway for this reason.

There is no way that you can mistake the busy signal for the high beeping tone if you remember this: the high beeping tone will not start until your party has answered their phone, which obviously is not true for a busy signal.

7. WEATHER AND DRESS

London weather in the summer is normally quite cool by American standards. It is not uncommon to need a sweater or even a coat or jacket at the height of summer. This cool weather is a great advantage for the visitor, since touring is much more comfortable in cooler weather. But you must bring, or expect to buy, clothes to keep you warm if the weather becomes very cool. Rain is frequent and sometimes unexpected. The experienced Londoner carries an umbrella on most days, even when the day starts out bright and cloudless, because the weather is very changeable. We advise that you purchase folding umbrellas and carry them with you on most days. You can buy these in London at Woolworth's (affectionately known as "Woolies") on Oxford Street as cheaply as you can in America. The weather has been somewhat abnormal recently. The summer of 1976 was the hottest and driest in several hundred years, and the summer of 1977 was the wettest in a hundred years (but don't let this discourage you from going, because there were still plenty of nice days and blue skies). The old peasoup fogs are a thing of the past because the burning of coal and wood is no longer permitted. If you have access to a radio or a TV set (called "the telly"), you will find the weather forecasts quite reliable for up to twenty-four hours ahead, and these can be very helpful in planning whether to do an indoor or an outdoor activity the following day.

London women wear dresses (rather more than in America) and slacks. Shorts are taboo. Pants suits are fine. London men wear business suits, sports jackets, and ties. Loud sports shirts are taboo. Jeans, especially Levis, are often worn for casual or informal occasions or for going to the grocery store.

8. MEDICAL AND DENTAL CARE

If you wish to see a general practitioner, you can get a list of the GPs (general practitioners) in your neighborhood who are affiliated with the National Health Service by asking at the post office in your area. The GP you see can then recommend a specialist if that seems advisable. Emergency service is provided by

Middlesex Hospital, Mortimer Street, W1

St. Mary's Hospital, Praed Street, W2

Westminster Hospital, Horseferry Road, SW1

An ambulance may be summoned by calling the city-wide emergency number 999 (no coins needed for this from a coin phone). *English medical care is of a high standard, comparable to and sometimes better than American care.*

If you need a dentist, you can find one in the Yellow Pages. Or the National Health Executive Council will recommend dentists. For dental emergencies, go to the emergency room of your local general hospital (they will dispense painkillers to help until you can see a dentist) or contact University College's Dental Hospital. But a word of warning: *English dental care is not up to American standards at all, and you are much better off if you can postpone all except emergency treatment until you get back to America.*

There is an all-night drugstore (called a "chemist's") in Piccadilly Circus called "Boots."

9. FINDING A PLACE TO STAY

You can reserve accommodations before leaving for London or you can find a place when you arrive. In either case, you can have the powerful assistance of the London Tourist Board, which is discussed later.

If you plan to stay for a week or two, you will want a hotel or a hostel. But if you plan to stay longer, you should look into the possibility of a furnished apartment (which is called a "flat"). In either case, stay in some part of Central London if you possibly can. Remember that you are there to see London and that you have limited time; if you take a place in the suburbs (for example, in Richmond), you are not likely to make the trip into Central London every day and might therefore waste precious time.

If you want to reserve a hotel in advance, get a copy of *Nicholson's London Guide* (see our Guide Book section below on how to order these in America). This book has an excellent list of hotels divided into three categories ("Luxury," "Medium Prices," and "Low Prices") with a brief description of each hotel. All of the hotels on their lists are in Central London. Write directly to the hotel to make a reservation. If the prices in *Nicholson's* low-priced group are not low enough for you, then get a copy of *Let's Go: Britain and Ireland* (from your local bookstore or by special order through them) which caters to traveling students. The gem of this book is its listing of inexpensive hotels and hostels for more than £1.50 per person with a pithy description of each, the list being divided by district: Bloomsbury, Earls Court, Paddington/Bayswater, and Victoria. Of these districts, we agree with the book's recommendation of Bloomsbury as the most desirable, since you are adjacent to the British Museum and Oxford Street and the West End on the one side and to the western edge of the City on the other side.

Free lists of London hotel rooms that can be reserved from the United States can be obtained by writing to the British Tourist Authority (680 Fifth Avenue, New York, N.Y. 10019; phone 212-581-4700).

If you are planning to stay for a couple of months or longer and wish to reserve a flat in advance, you can write directly to real estate agents (called "estate agents") who specialize in short-term rentals or in "holiday lets." Here are the addresses and phone numbers of several of these agents:

> Around Town Flats Ltd., 120 Holland Park Avenue, London W 11 (01-229-0033)
>
> Phillips, Kay & Lewis, 56 Grosvenor Street, London W1 (01-629-8811)
>
> James & Jacobs, 94 Jermyn Street, London SW1 (01-930-0261)
>
> Abbey Ltd., 315 Maddox Street, London W1 (01-493-9251)
>
> George Knight & Partners, 9 Heath Street, London NW3 (01-794-1125)
>
> Ferrier & Davies, 6 Beauchamp Place, London SW3 (01-584-3232)

Some agents handling properties of this type will send you lists of what they have available; others may prefer to rent only to people already in town. There are a relatively large number of short-term flat rentals available because of the structure of English rent laws. These rent laws make it very difficult under certain circumstances for a landlord to evict a long-term tenant. Therefore, an apartment owner who will be out of England for a short period and wants his or her apartment back upon returning will prefer to rent to a foreigner who will be leaving England at a definite time.

A holiday let will normally be an apartment or house (or even, if you are lucky, a houseboat). There is another category of apartments, called "serviced flats." These are usually in residential hotels and offer the usual kitchen, bathroom, and one or more bedrooms together with laundry service, television and telephone, maid service, linen and towels, and so on. The British Tourist Authority will provide a list of fully serviced flats upon request. Another source of serviced flats is the classified ad section in the magazine *In Britain,* published monthly by the British Tourist Authority. Write to the BTA for a packet of tourist materials and they will normally include a free copy of this magazine. Or you can subscribe to the magazine by writing to Box 508, Allwood, Clifton, New Jersey, 07012.

These are ways of reserving accommodations before you arrive in London. Should you do this? Is it necessary to do this? The advantage of doing so is obvious: you will definitely have a place to stay when you get there. This is no small consideration. During several days in July 1977, the London Tourist Board, who are aces at finding accommodations for visitors, ran out of rooms and had to house people in such unlikely places as the crypts of churches. This is admittedly unusual. The disadvantage of reserving a place from America is that you will not have seen the place that you have reserved and you may not like it when you see it. Moreover, when you arrive in London, you may be able to find something nice for less money.

Now, let's suppose that you arrive in London without reservations. Then you can call the hotels listed in *Nicholson's* or in *Let's Go: Britain and Ireland.* If you are looking for a holiday let, you can call the estate agents listed above; you can also consult the classified ads on the last page of *The London Times,* a daily morning newspaper. If all else fails or if you prefer to have help in finding a hotel, let the London Tourist Board work their magic for you. Here is what the Board says about its services:

Hotel Accommodation Service. To book, go on the day accommodations are required to the Tourist Information Centre at Victoria Station (near Platform 15, open 8 AM to 10:30 PM from mid-May to September, closing earlier during the winter months). A £2 deposit, deductible from the final hotel bill, must be paid at the time of reservation. Advance bookings are handled by letter from the Board's Head Office (London Tourist Board, 26 Grosvenor Gardens, London SW1 ODU); please send inquiries four weeks in advance of the date of arrival to this address. We can provide accommodation in a wide range of price categories in over 800 hotels and guest houses within a twenty mile radius of Central London.

Budget Accommodation Service. We offer budget accommodation in hostels, dormitories, and pensions. Prices range from £2.50 per day (sharing) to £4.00 (single). Central London locations are more expensive than those in the suburbs. To book, go on the day accommodation is required to the Victoria Station Tourist Information Centre. A booking fee of 35p (value-added tax inclusive) per person is charged. Advance bookings are handled through the Board's Head Office. Applications should be made at least six weeks in advance.

10. SAFETY

You must remember that automobiles in England drive on the left-hand side of the road. So you must look to your *right* for cars as you wait at the curb to cross the street. This is no light matter, especially in London where the traffic is often fast and heavy. There are exceptions to this rule, particularly on one-way streets; and in such cases you will often find signs on the surface of the street beside the curb telling you which way to look.

Electrical power in England carries 240 volts, twice as much as in America. Most visitors know that this means that they should bring converters for their electric razors and radios (or else use battery-operated equipment). But many visitors do not realize that this voltage can give the careless person a very healthy jolt and in some circumstances can be quite dangerous. Electrical wall sockets in England are equipped with switches on their face plates. The proper procedure for plugging an appliance into the socket is this: first, turn off the socket by setting its switch so that the red dot on the top of the switch does not show; then plug in the appliance; finally, turn on the switch so that the red dot does show. If you plug in an appliance and it won't work, check to see that the socket is turned on at its own switch.

11. NAMES FOR PARTS OF LONDON

London is a collection of towns and villages that gradually flowed together over the years to form one great metropolitan area. At the beginning of this century the London area was divided into twenty-eight boroughs and was under the general supervision of the London County Council. In 1965 the Greater London area was reorganized and is now governed by the Greater London Council (the GLC). The names of the old villages, districts, and boroughs persist in everyday use, including Mayfair, St. James's, Soho, Paddington, Bloomsbury, Kensington, Belgravia, and Pimlico.

The expression "the West End" refers roughly to the area from Knightsbridge and Kensington in the southwest, Paddington in the northwest, Marylebone and Regent's Park on the north, and Charing Cross Road and Tottenham Court Road on the east. (This expression is colloquial, and people will disagree about the exact boundaries of the West End. For example, some will say that the West End begins at Marble Arch.) The West End contains the legislative and administrative branches of government, the fashionable shopping areas of Knightsbridge, Oxford Street, and New Bond Street, and the theater district.

Moving east from the West End, we encounter the areas known as Bloomsbury, Holborn, the Strand, and Covent Garden. Moving further east, we come to the City of London. This expression "the City of London" is the name of the present financial district of London. This district is the old London of Roman and medieval times and is sometimes called "the Square Mile." It extends from Fleet Street on the west, Smithfield Market, Barbican, and Liverpool Street Station on the north, to Middlesex Street and the Tower of London on the east, with the Thames as its southern boundary. It is this area that is often called simply "the City." Thus, London and the City of London must not be confused with one another; the latter is only a part of the former.

The East End consists of the areas east of the City of London, such as Whitechapel, Spitalfields, Stepney, and Bethnal Green.

It is important not to confuse Westminster (which is the area immediately around the Houses of Parliament and Westminster Abbey) with the City of Westminster (which is an administrative unit covering roughly much of the area west of the City of London, including the West End).

All that we have spoken of so far lies on the North Bank of the Thames. The South Bank includes such areas as Southwark, Lambeth, and Clapham. There are a few places of interest to visitors on the South Bank, and we will indicate some of these later; but most places of interest are on the North Bank.

12. RADIO AND TELEVISION

British television has three channels: BBC 1, BBC 2, and ITV (Independent Television). The BBC (British Broadcasting Corporation) channels are supported by the government and are therefore entirely free of commercials. Enjoy a full-length movie without any interruptions for ads! The BBC produces "Masterpiece Theater," "The Duchess of Duke Street," and other series that brighten our screens in America. ITV consists of different companies that provide service to different regions of Great Britain (in London the company is called Thames Television). Sets usually have pushbuttons, which are pretuned to these three channels.

There is no publication in England equivalent to our *TV Guide,* listing all the programs on all the channels for the whole week. In order to get week-long schedules for both BBC and ITV, you have to buy two separate magazines each week: *Radio Times* for the BBC schedule, and *TV Times* for the ITV schedule. These magazines usually go on sale at news-agents shops (where you buy your newspapers) on Wednesday for the following week. You can also find each day's programs listed in the newspapers for that day; the Sunday papers do *not* carry the week's schedule.

Radio Times also lists the weekly schedules for the BBC radio service. And radio schedules are also carried one day at a time by the daily newspapers.

13. FLOORS

What Americans call the "first floor" the English call the "ground floor." And what Americans call the "second floor" the English call the "first floor." This difference can be important in selecting your hotel room or in going to visit someone. If you are given a third-floor room in a hotel, and there is no elevator (or "lift"), then you can expect to climb up and down *three* flights of stairs, not two.

14. SHOPPING

Oxford Street from Marble Arch to Tottenham Court Road is the great shopping street in London. It contains department stores and some specialty shops. Marks & Spencer is well-known world-wide for giving good value. Selfridges is also very good. We especially recommend John Lewis (on the north side of Oxford Street, just west of Oxford Circus); it has many good departments, including clothes, knitting yarns and fabrics, and a fine toy department. A number of other good department stores—for example, Dickens & Jones, and Liberty—are located in Regent Street, as is the enormous toy store Hamley's. Harrods, in Knightsbridge, is vast and has everything—including high prices. Our advice

GENERAL INFORMATION AND ADVICE

is to look at Harrods and buy at John Lewis or Marks & Spencer.

Old Bond Street and New Bond Street have block after block of expensive specialty shops, including most of the famous names in high fashion. Savile Row is famous for men's tailoring. The King's Road in Chelsea, Tottenham Court Road, and the Edgware Road are other large-scale shopping streets.

If you are looking for a particular type of item, then consult the section on "Shopping" in *Nicholson's London Guide*. It gives an excellent list of shops broken down by specialty categories.

There are a number of street markets in London, Portobello Road and Petticoat Lane perhaps being the most famous. Petticoat Lane (Middlesex Street, near Liverpool Street Station) is open only on Sundays. *Do not go* to Petticoat Lane—unless you want to be crushed in a mob of tourists and swept along with little chance of seeing any of the merchandise. If you want to see the markets at which Londoners themselves shop in order to stretch the pound, visit the Leather Lane Market (between Clerkenwell and Holborn, Chancery Lane tube) or the Berwick (pronounced "barrack") Street Market (running south from Oxford Street in Soho, Oxford Circus tube). The Berwick Street Market is particularly good for fruit and vegetables at more reasonable prices than you will find in most grocery stores.

We also recommend the Drury Coffee Company (3 New Row, off St. Martin's Lane, Leicester Square tube) for excellent coffee beans and tea. You *can* buy good coffee in England—at Drury's.

15. 35mm PHOTOGRAPHY

If you use Kodak 35mm film, there is no need to bring film from America. Kodak 35mm film is sold everywhere in London; and if you take a little trouble, you can find it discounted so that the film and processing turns out to be cheaper than it is in America. For example, in the summer of 1977, 36-exposure Kodachrome 64 could be found for £3.15 to £3.35 including processing. We recommend that you buy your film at Boots Chemists (many branches in London); they sell it even more cheaply than do the photographic shops.

But there is a problem about using English Kodak processing, namely that while it is very good in quality—certainly the equal of American Kodak processing—it is too slow for someone who is staying only two or three weeks. It often takes two or three weeks (partly because the mails tend to be slow) to get processed film back from the Kodak plant at Hemel Hempstead. So our advice is to bring your exposed film and mailers back to America and mail them to your nearest Kodak developing plant here. The mailers that you buy in England are perfectly valid in America too. Be sure to hand your exposed film separately to the security baggage inspector at Heathrow or Gatwick when you board; they are very good about not putting it through their electronic inspection machines.

16. ARCHITECTURE

One's pleasure in visiting London is greatly enhanced by an acquaintance with the main historical styles of architecture. Fortunately there is a way for a person who has no knowledge of architecture to gain this knowledge of styles both pleasantly and rapidly. Buy a copy of *The Observer's Book of Architecture* by John Penoyre and Michael Ryan (published by Frederick Warne and Co., Ltd., London and distributed in the U.S. by Charles Scribner's Sons, New York). This book is very short but an absolute marvel of its kind and costs only a little more than £1 in London and $2.95 in America. It is a superb survey of English architecture, explaining the origin and rationale of each style and relating each style to the society in which it developed. One invaluable feature of the book is a set of diagrams in the back which illustrate each style as to columns, ceilings, doorways, windows, and general character; these drawings are very effective in helping one to recognize what one is seeing. This book is easily obtained from major bookstores (see our section on bookstores below). We also recommend that you consider purchasing two other inexpensive books: *The Observer's Book of Cathedrals* (also published by Warne; see especially chapters 1–3), and *Discovering Churches* by John Harries (Shire Publications), both of which nicely supplement Penoyre and Ryan with excellent text and diagrams.

The following is a list of the principal architectural styles in England, their dates, and a few examples to be found in London:

Saxon (700–1070)

Norman (1070–1150): St. Bartholomew the Great; St. John's Chapel in the White Tower, at the Tower of London; parts of Southwark Cathedral

Transitional (1150–90): The Temple Church

Early English (1190–1280): Westminster Abbey (the nave); Southwark Cathedral (the Retrochoir)

Decorated (1280–1360): St. Mary Abbotts, Kensington

Perpendicular (1360–1480): Henry VII Chapel in Westminster Abbey

Tudor (1480–1600): Staple Inn; Prince Henry's Room

Jacobean (1600–50): Queen's House, Greenwich; Banqueting House, Whitehall; 59–60 Lincoln's Inn Fields

Restoration (1650–1700): St. Paul's Cathedral; the Royal Naval College, Greenwich

Queen Anne (1700–15): The houses in Queen Anne's Gate; Dr. Samuel Johnson's House in Gough Square

Georgian (1720–1810): Bedford Square; Harley Street and Wimpole Street

Regency (1810–30): the Nash Terraces around Regent's Park; Regency balconies at One Dorset Square; at the northwest corner of Devonshire Street and Harley Street; at the extreme west end of Pall Mall

Victorian (1830–1900): Hotel Russell; Dillon's Bookstore; Paddington Rail Station

One word of warning: It is very difficult to tell the age of a building in London merely from its architectural style. The Victorian architects were extremely skilled at imitating earlier styles, in addition to building in their own styles. Thus, a building which is clearly in the Queen Anne style may turn out to have been built in the nineteenth century rather than at the beginning of the eighteenth century.

17. BOOKSTORES

It pays Americans to buy books in England that are published originally in England, since they are significantly lower in price than the equivalent American editions. This is one of the ways in which England remains a bargain for Americans. For example, a recent best-selling English novel which sold for $12.95 in America cost just under $9 in England. (Naturally one's savings depend on the exchange rate, which does fluctuate.)

Hatchards (187 Piccadilly, Piccadilly Circus or Green Park tube) is an excellent bookstore with a high-quality, general stock, specializing in personal service. If they do not have what you are looking for, they will suggest other sources. (And their shop has delightful eighteenth-century bow windows.) Mowbray's (28 Margaret Street, Oxford Circus tube) is of similar quality and somewhat larger. Foyles (119–125 Charing Cross Road, Tottenham Court Road tube) is said to be the largest bookstore in England. Dillon's (1 Malet Street, Goodge Street tube) serves the University of London and is superb for academic and scholarly books.

There are quite a few used-book shops but they are not of the quality and quantity that one would expect of a metropolis like London. Furthermore, their prices are quite high, often around three-quarters of the price of the new book. A number of used-book shops are in Charing Cross Road, particularly between Oxford Street and Leicester Square, but better-quality shops are to be found in St. Martin's Court and in Cecil Court off Charing Cross Road just below Leicester Square. A center of used books is also emerging in Sackville Street (north side of Piccadilly, between Piccadilly Circus and New Bond Street).

Many bookshops carry stocks of remainder books (new books at greatly reduced prices). Some of the best of these are the various Claude Gill shops (especially 481 Oxford Street) and the Booksmith shops (on St. Martin's Lane next to the north side of the London Coliseum, and on Charing Cross Road just below Oxford Street).

If you want to buy books but find yourself short of cash, open a charge account at Dillon's (at the accounts window on the ground floor). Then choose your books and tell the salesperson that you have opened an account. They will hold your selections until the account is approved (usually about four weeks) and then will mail them (by sea mail, unless you specify air mail) to your American address.

18. STREET NUMBERING

On quite a few streets, the street numbers are consecutive rather than odd numbers on one side and even numbers on the other. Moreover, you will find that the numbers go consecutively down one side and then back up the other side, so that if you are standing in front of Number 39, the house across the street might be numbered 142.

Some houses and buildings that are on side streets leading off a main street will have a street address on that main street. You will have to look down a side street for the building itself.

Occasionally, a street address will list two streets, like this: 40 Hallam Street, Portland Place. Portland Place is listed to tell you roughly where Hallam Street is, because Portland Place is a very well-known street. (In this example, Hallam Street runs parallel to Portland Place and one block to the west.) Nicholson's, the guide-book publishers, list themselves at "Goodwin's Court, St. Martin's Place" because Goodwin's Court can be exceedingly hard to find.

19.   PUBS

You don't have to drink an alcoholic beverage to be welcome at a pub (short for "public house"). You can order a "lemonade" and get what Americans would call a bitter lemon. So don't let lack of interest in drinking prevent you from spending a little time in a pub now and then. Many Englishmen show up regularly at their "local" to see their friends and relax in a friendly atmosphere. (And, correspondingly, people entertain each other in their homes less than do Americans.) You will want to see some pubs not only to observe the English at leisure but also for the sake of the interior decor—particularly the brass, mirrors, and polished wood of the Victorian pubs. Many pubs serve light meals.

One of the nicest ways for an American to see some pubs is to go on one of *London Walks'* "Historic London Pub Walks" or one of their "Real Ale Walks." (See our section below on guides and guide books for further information about *London Walks*.)

20. THEATER, CONCERTS, AND OPERA

The theater in London is probably the best in the world. The National Theatre on the South Bank may have the consistently highest standard, but many theaters in the West End regularly present splendid performances of the classics and of modern plays. After touring London during the day, go to a play (or a concert) in the evening.

If you are in London for only a couple of weeks, you will not want to spend your time traveling to the box offices of individual theaters to purchase tickets (unless you happen to be in the neighborhood anyway); you have more important and gratifying things to do with your time. Our advice is to buy your tickets from a ticket broker. Keith Prowse is the largest broker with many branches around town, and we have found their staff to be efficient, knowledgeable, and reliable. Look in the Yellow Pages for the branch nearest you. Every broker charges a small commission on each ticket, but they save you much time. And, just as important, they can give you advice on what is worth seeing and which seats are good. There are some theaters (similar to our off-Broadway theaters) for which you cannot get tickets through a broker; but they do handle tickets for most of the West End theaters, many concert halls, the two opera companies, and the ballet. In many theaters, you can use your broker's receipt as your ticket without having to queue at the box office to pick up your tickets when you get to the theater. Keith Prowse branches have seating charts and brochures and will take almost any credit card.

An attractive feature of the London theatrical scene is that plays and concerts generally begin earlier than in America, often at 7:30 P.M. This allows time for dinner after the show and then getting home by tube before the tube closes around midnight. English theaters charge extra for programs, usually 20p to 30p each. During intermission, red and white wine are usually available, along with ice cream in various forms. (Americans will find English ice cream very disappointing—thin and watery—because it is made with vegetable oil rather than with cream. But there is no truth to the rumor that English ice cream is made with leftover school paste and reduced pigs trotters!)

Here are some of our special recommendations. The Young Vic Company (no relation to the Old Vic nearby) gives excellent, exciting productions at extremely modest prices (all seats about £1). English theater is still cheap by American standards, but it is no longer dirt cheap, and the Young Vic offers very good value as an exception to the rise in prices. (To get to the Young Vic, get off at Waterloo tube station, coming out on York Road, turn right to Waterloo Road and right again to go down Waterloo Road, then turn left at The Cut—opposite the Old Vic; the Young Vic is about 200 yards further on the north side of the street.) The Open Air Theatre in Regent's Park puts on excellent Shakespeare and other drama in a sylvan setting during the summer (Baker Street or Regent's Park tube to Queen Mary's Rose Garden in the park).

For concerts, the Queen Elizabeth Hall is the prestige hall for soloists and small groups, while the Royal Festival Hall fulfills the same role for larger music and dance groups. Both are located in the South Bank Arts Center next to the National Theatre. (Get off at Waterloo tube, then go by ramp across York Road.) All of these halls on the South Bank have a priceless feature beyond the performances themselves, namely that during intermission you can walk out on their balconies and terraces and enjoy a glorious view of the Thames riverfront at night—with the Houses of Parliament and Big Ben lit up on your left and St. Paul's and the City aglow on your right.

High-quality but very inexpensive solo and chamber music concerts are given at the Wigmore Hall (Bond Street or Oxford Circus tube). This hall presents a concert every night of the week and twice on Sundays, and at their prices (usually ranging from 60p to a top of £1.80), you can afford to go to every concert. Wigmore Hall acoustics are superb, so feel free to sit in the back for 60p.

The internationally famous opera house in London is the Royal Opera House in Covent Garden (Covent Garden tube). This is where Joan Sutherland, Placido Domingo, and the other great stars of opera appear. The Covent Garden season begins late in September and demand for tickets is extremely heavy. You can buy tickets by mail, so before leaving America, write to them for a brochure (Royal Opera House, Covent Garden, London WC2) and then order by using the forms that they send you. Prices range from £1 to £15, but it is very difficult to get lower-price seats unless you queue at the box office when the booking season opens or else are very fortunate with your mail order. Opera buffs should also attend the English National Opera (Trafalgar Square tube) at the London Coliseum, which, without benefit of international stars, has been going "from triumph to triumph," as Andrew Porter, the opera critic for *The New Yorker,* has rightly said. The ENO gives excellent performances, often as good as or better than Covent Garden and at much more reasonable prices (a top of about £6). All ENO productions are in English and include the standard repertoire (Verdi, Mozart, Wagner), operettas, and contemporary opera. After the opera, walk into a floodlit Trafalgar Square, one of the handsomest nocturnal urban settings in the world.

So our message is this: by choosing carefully and focusing on such companies as the Young Vic, Wigmore Hall, and the ENO, you can still enjoy superior performances at low prices in London; but in general prices are still not extremely high at other theaters and you should go if you can possibly afford it.

A final word on booking tickets: Keith Prowse also has a branch in New York City and they may be able to help you arrange tickets before you leave America (1345 Avenue of the Americas, New York, N.Y. 10019; phone 212-581-1400).

21. OUR GUIDE TO GUIDE BOOKS AND GUIDES

The year 1977 was a great one for London visitors because in August 1977 the first edition of the *Michelin Green Guide to London* in English was published. Its appearance was greeted with a front-page article in *The London Times,* which noted with satisfaction that London has more three-star sights in the French-based Michelin guides than does Paris itself.

We believe that the minimum or basic equipment (besides money and a copy of this book) for a visitor to London is a copy of the *Michelin Green Guide,* a copy of *Nicholson's London Guide,* and a copy of Tom Pocock's *London Walks.*

The *Michelin Green Guide* is not to be confused with Michelin red guides to restaurants and hotels. The *Green Guide* describes places of interest in detail, giving much historical background and, in many cases, maps. It gives floor plans of museums and lists of their collections. The fold-out map in the front of the book has a map of Central London on one side on far too large a scale to be useful for navigating; but on the back of this fold-out map is a map of the City (remember: the City is the financial district), which is the finest available and invaluable to the visitor in negotiating the maze of City streets. There are also short but helpful sections on the growth and government of London and on architecture.

Nicholson's London Guide is a thin, pocket-size book that is a gold mine of information. It has street maps of Central London keyed to a street index, shopping and theater maps, tube and bus maps, and lists, lists, lists of historic buildings, statues, churches, museums and parks, children's sights, hotels, restaurants, pubs, night clubs, theaters, and a shopping section divided by type of item. It is amazing how much information is crammed into this little book. Many Londoners carry this guide with them. One pays a price for all this—the print is very small and the clarity of the printing has deteriorated markedly over the years. If you have trouble reading small print, never fear—you can buy exactly the same book in a very large, easy-to-read format called *Nicholson's Complete London*. This is the deluxe edition of the pocket guide; what you lose in portability you gain in legibility. The difference in price between the two editions is about £1.20. (Both Nicholson's guides are distributed in the United States by Charles Scribner's Sons, New York.)

Another book that we strongly recommend is Tom Pocock's *London Walks* (Arco Publishing Co., New York). This inexpensive book gives thirty easy walks in Central London and the outskirts. Each walk is accompanied by a small map to help you find your way and a chatty, informative text that conveys a sense of the city's life. George W. Oakes's *Turn Right at the Fountain* (Holt, Rinehart and Winston, New York) contains four long walks in London: "The City—West," "The City—East," "Westminster," and "Chelsea-Kensington." When Oakes's book appeared in 1965, these walks were the best things of their kind—and the book is still invaluable for its walks in other European cities, including Edinburgh, Amsterdam, Rome, Paris, Vienna, Athens, Barcelona, and so on. If your stay in London is only one part of a longer European trip, then get Oakes's book for the other cities. But for London, we feel that Pocock's *London Walks* supersedes Oakes's book. Pocock, a native Londoner, has many stories to tell and imparts a true feeling for London as only a Londoner could do. His book contains many walks, covers many areas of the city, and the walks are shorter than Oakes's, so that one is not led to try to see too much at once. However, we heartily endorse Oakes's view that "you cannot see a city properly, particularly in Europe, unless you do it on foot," and we strongly recommend his companion volume *Turn Left at the Pub,* a fine collection of walks in other English towns such as Bath, Canterbury, and Oxford.

For those students of the city who wish even more detail than Michelin provides, two excellent books are available, the *Blue Guide to London* (now published in paperback by Ernest Benn at £2.50) and the *Penguin Guide to London* by F. R. Banks (£1.50). These give almost a block-by-block description of London, including some outlying areas. They are encyclopedic but are small enough to be carried by the serious student on forays through town. The *Encyclopaedia of London* by William Kent (published by J. M. Dent) is vastly informative too, being over twice the size of the *Blue Guide* and the *Penguin Guide,* and is just what you need to explore the history of the city in great detail. Unfortunately, Kent's book is now out of print (only temporarily, we hope); if you find a copy in a bookstore, snap it up.

Two other books are worth mentioning. *Discovering London for Children* by Margaret Pearson (Shire Publications) is not just for children. It gives very interesting tours of Westminster Abbey, the Tower of London, and twenty-three other points of interest; it is full of tales and facts and well worth its very modest price. *Blimy! Another Book About London* by Donald Goddard (published by Johnston and Bacon) gives a remarkable portrait of the attitudes and life-style of Londoners that will help you to understand the people that you meet.

Many visitors to London buy a street atlas. This is not necessary for Central London, since *Nicholson's London Guide* will handle all questions about that area. But if you venture into the suburbs, you may require a Greater London street atlas. Most people buy *London A to Z,* but we prefer *Nicholson's London Street Finder* because it is more legible and easier to use. The A-to-Z people, though, do put out separate maps that are very helpful, and their London Super Scale

GENERAL INFORMATION AND ADVICE 31

Map is a thing of beauty and a delight to the connoisseur of London.

These guide books are available at the larger bookstores in London. Some of them (including *Nicholson's London Guide, Penguin Guide to London, Blue Guide to London, Discovering London for Children,* and *A–Z London Super Scale Map,* as well as Pocock's *London Walks*) are available in America through the British Travel Bookshop Ltd., 680 Fifth Avenue, New York, N.Y. 10019. Write to them for their catalog.

We have a special recommendation to make about guides. There is an organization now operating in London called London Walks (not to be confused with the book *London Walks*). They provide guided walks all year round, and we *strongly* urge you to take one or more of their walks. These walks include "A Journey Through Dickens' London," "Legal and Illegal London," "Sir Christopher Wren's London," "Ghosts of the City," "A Historical London Pub Walk—Chelsea," and "Discovering London: Bloomsbury." These are only samples of a wide variety of types of walks and areas of the city covered. We have taken a number of these walks and have found them to be of superior quality, uniformly interesting, and with knowledgeable and articulate guides who obviously love London and who have a great wealth of facts to convey and tales to tell. You rendezvous with your guide at the listed underground station at the time indicated on the London Walks schedule. Your guide is the man or woman carrying a portfolio and wearing an expectant look just outside the main entrance to the tube station. (Some of the guides also wear the little lapel badge of a registered guide.) Each walk lasts about two hours, goes on rain or shine, and in general ends at another tube station. (The pub walks last about three hours and visit four or five pubs.) The fee for a walk is 80p per person (children under fourteen free). This is dirt cheap for what you get—and even then a discount ticket is available at £2 for four walks. The organization says:

> Walkabout tickets, information on the walks, and future programmes can be obtained by sending a stamped, self-addressed envelope to 139 Conway Road, London N14. When writing from abroad, it would be appreciated if an international reply coupon (obtainable from post offices) could be enclosed with the request for information. For telephone enquiries, call us on 882-2763.

The schedules put out by the organization cover five or six months at a time, so it is possible for you to send away from America and get a schedule covering your visit before you leave for England.

Several of the museums offer lectures and gallery talks on their collections. The British Museum offers both, usually one lecture and one gallery talk each day. Schedules may be picked up at the information desk in the main entrance hall (off Great Russell Street) or at the North Entrance desk (off Montague Place). Topics range from Greek vases and the royal tombs of Ur to Britain in the Bronze Age and Chinese ceramics. The National Gallery offers lectures ranging from the Umbrian painters of the Renaissance to Romanticism and English landscape. A lecture is given every day but Sundays and Fridays, usually at 1 P.M. (Saturdays at 12). Brochures on the lectures are available in the front entrance hall. The Wallace Collection offers gallery talks on Wednesdays at 1 P.M. and Fridays at 2:30 P.M., dealing with such subjects as Watteau, Rembrandt and Hals, French furniture, and Sèvres porcelain. Schedules of these talks may be picked up at the postcard sales desk to the left of the main entrance hall. All of these lectures and talks are free of charge, and we recommend them very highly. They are a splendid way of getting to know parts of these collections in detail and of expanding one's own artistic sensitivity.

Many of the places of interest in London sell guide books for those places, containing glorious color photographs and more information than in the Michelin, Penguin, or Blue

GENERAL INFORMATION AND ADVICE 33

guides. Those booklets published by the British Government—and in fact almost everything else published by the government—can also be purchased at Her Majesty's Stationery Office Bookshop at 49 High Holborn (Holborn tube). Those which are privately published—such as the Pitkin and Jarrold guides—can also be purchased at Hatchards, Mowbray's, and other good bookstores.

The London Tourist Board has information centers

> At Victoria Station (near Platform 15)
>
> At 26 Grosvenor Gardens, SW1
>
> In Selfridges Department Store, Oxford Street, W1, on the ground floor
>
> In Harrods Department Store, Knightsbridge, SW3, on the fourth floor
>
> At the Tower of London

At these centers you can have your questions answered and get information on sightseeing tours, excursions from London, river trips on the Thames, publications, and tourist tickets.

The City of London Information Center (01-606-3030) is located in St. Paul's Churchyard, on the south side of St. Paul's Cathedral. It has information on places of interest and events in the square mile of the City of London.

Finally, if you are interested in Roman London, get the splendid and inexpensive booklet *A Handbook to Roman London* at the Museum of London. You can give yourself a tour of Roman London by using the centerfold map.

Part Two

SUGGESTED SCHEDULES

In this section we give you schedules that illustrate how your visiting might be arranged. These schedules are intended to help you avoid the mistake made by so many visitors of concentrating on one type of activity—major places of interest only or shopping only—by giving examples of how quite a number of activities can be put together even within a single week. Our schedules attempt to provide variety, alternating a visit to a major place of interest with a walk, followed by a day at an important place outside London, followed by a visit to a museum, and so on. Naturally, during the first week, we list quite a few major places of interest, on the principle that if you have only one week to spend in London, there are certain places that you must not miss, even at the price of eliminating some variety from the schedule.

These schedules are intended to be cumulative, so that no one of them repeats anything on the others (except for two repeat visits to some museums). If you actually follow these schedules as listed, you will see a hundred times more of London than do most visitors.

We assume that you are armed with copies of the *Michelin*

Green Guide, Nicholson's London Guide (or the *Complete London*), and Tom Pocock's *London Walks*.

Naturally, these are only suggestions, and you should make substitutions based on your own particular interests.

1. FIRST WEEK SCHEDULE

First Day:

Morning: Houses of Parliament and Westminster Abbey
Afternoon: Pocock's walk in St. James's

Second Day:

Morning: The National Gallery
Afternoon: Our walk Number 11: The Strand, St. Martin's Lane, and Covent Garden (see Part Five)

Third Day:

Spend the whole day at Hampton Court.

Fourth Day:

Morning: Shopping in New Bond Street and Oxford Street
Afternoon: The British Museum

Fifth Day:

Spend the whole day at Greenwich.

Sixth Day:

Morning: Our walk Number 12: Legal London
Afternoon: The Wallace Collection

Seventh Day:

Morning: The Tower of London
Afternoon: St. Paul's Cathedral

Notes: (1) The Houses of Parliament may not be open to visitors when you are there; be sure to check the times of opening in the Michelin Green Guide; *(2) On the St. James's walk, be sure to look for Pickering Place, which Pocock unaccountably does not mention.*

2. SECOND WEEK SCHEDULE

First Day:

Morning: The National Portrait Gallery
Afternoon: Our walk Number 13: A City Church Walk

Second Day:

Spend the whole day at Windsor Castle.

Third Day:

Morning: Our walk Number 3: Southwark and London Bridge
Afternoon: A walk with the organization London Walks

Fourth Day:

Morning: The Tate Gallery
Afternoon: Our walk Number 15: Marylebone

Fifth Day:

Spend the whole day at Kew Gardens.

Sixth Day:

Morning: Pocock's Chelsea walk
Afternoon: The Victoria and Albert Museum

Seventh Day:

Morning: Kensington Palace
Afternoon: Our walk Number 4: Bloomsbury Squares and Museums

3. THIRD WEEK SCHEDULE

First Day:

Morning: Pocock's walk "The Fleet Street Story"
Afternoon: The Museum of London and St. Bartholomew the Great (see our walk Number 5)

Second Day:

Spend the day in Hampstead and Highgate (see Pocock's walks for these) and at Kenwood House.

Third Day:

Morning: More shopping
Afternoon: Our walk Number 7: A Walk Around Regent's Park

Fourth Day:

Morning: Second visit to the Victoria and Albert Museum
Afternoon: A walk in Soho (our Number 18 or Pocock's)

Fifth Day:

Morning: Our walk Number 10: St. James's Park, Queen Anne's Gate, and Banqueting House
Afternoon: Second visit to the National Gallery

Sixth Day:

Spend the day seeing Hatfield House (see Part Four).

Seventh Day:

Morning: Our walk Number 19: Knightsbridge and South Kensington
Afternoon: Our walk Number 6: Across the Thames from the South Bank Arts Centre

Part Three

MAJOR PLACES OF INTEREST

In this part we deal with the places of major importance that (with one exception) every visitor will want to see. We will not describe these in detail because one of your other guide books will do this quite well. Instead, we concentrate on giving advice and tips on how to see these places.

1. THE BRITISH MUSEUM

The British Museum contains Greek, Roman, Near Eastern, Eastern, and English antiquities, plus prints and drawings, and the British Library. It is huge and inexhaustible. The visitor who is in London for only a short time must not try to see it all but must instead choose to see some parts and omit others. Here is our suggested tour which takes in many of the essential items.

Enter from Great Russell Street into the main entrance hall; turn left into the Assyrian Transept and then right into the Egyptian Sculpture Gallery (Room 25) to (1) the Rosetta Stone. Then from the middle of the Egyptian Sculpture Gallery, turn left through Rooms 15 and 7 into the Duveen Gallery for (2) the Elgin Marbles (and be sure to see the model of the Parthenon in a room just south of the entrance to this gallery). The *Blue Guide* (pages 182–83) and the *Penguin Guide* (pages 335–37) give excellent descriptions of the Marbles, their history, and what they represent. Then go back through the entrance to the Duveen Gallery into Room 7 to see (3) the Nereid Monument (which is the façade of a tomb reconstructed in the Museum). Go behind the Nereid Monument to (4) various Greek and Roman antiquities in Rooms 9 through 15. Next, go back the way you came, across the main entrance hall to the Manuscript Saloon and the King's Library for (5) rare manuscripts, including Magna Charta, Gutenberg bibles, books by the early printer Caxton, and a wide variety of incunabula. At the north end of the King's Library, ascend a short flight of stairs, turn left down a long passageway to the King Edward VII Gallery and (6) Chinese stoneware and porcelain, Asian bronzes and sculpture, and Turkish pottery. Taking the stairs or the lift to the upper floor of this gallery, you will find (7) prints and drawings by Michelangelo, Rubens, and Rembrandt. Then go through the Coptic Corridor to the Upper Egyptian galleries (Rooms 60–65) and (8) the Egyptian Mummies. Next, go to Rooms 54–51, through the Special Exhibitions Rooms (stopping to see what is on exhibit) and reaching Rooms 41–42 and (9) the Sutton Hoo Treasure. To leave, go through Room 40 to the Central Saloon and you will find the stairs or lift to the ground floor and the main entrance hall.

Unlike other museums in London, the British Museum permits photography. The book and postcard shops are off the main entrance hall.

2. THE HOUSES OF PARLIAMENT

The building that contains the Houses of Parliament is called the Palace of Westminster. This building also contains Westminster Hall (originally Norman, reconstructed in the fourteenth century).

Our advice about seeing this building is this: if you know the basic structure and functions of Parliament—if you know what a division lobby is, what the woolsack is, what powers the Lords have—then don't bother to take the guided tour (which begins at the base of the Victoria Tower); instead give yourself a tour by following the description of the interior given in the *Michelin Green Guide;* otherwise, take the tour. The difficulty with taking the tour is that, although it is inexpensive and adequately informative, it goes too fast past places in which you will want to linger.

There is one important point that many guide books do not mention but which must be understood in order to understand some features of the Houses of Parliament: the visitor's route is the route the sovereign takes when coming to address Parliament; the sovereign's throne is located in the House of Lords because no sovereign is allowed to enter the House of Commons, a remnant of past conflicts between king and Parliament; when the sovereign opens Parliament, the members of the Commons stand at the other end of the House of Lords.

If you guide yourself, do not miss Westminster Hall. Its dimensions are 240 feet by 70 feet with no internal supporting pillars, and it has a marvelous hammerbeam roof. People are divided as to whether this roof is the finest hammerbeam in existence or whether that distinction belongs to the roof of the Great Hall at Hampton Court. See them both! For excellent diagrams of hammerbeam and other roof construction, see John Harries, *Discovering Churches* (Shire Publications), page 53.

Before going to Westminster, check to see whether Parliament is open to visitors by calling the London Tourist Board at 730-0791. Normally (when sitting) Parliament is open for visitors only on Saturdays, except in August when it is open three days a week. Westminster Hall is open every day (except Sunday) when Parliament is not sitting, and in the mornings when Parliament is sitting. It is sometimes possible for a few Americans to attend Parliamentary sessions; apply to the American Embassy for information and passes. How to get there: After arriving at Westminster tube station, walk on Bridge Street away from the river, then left down St. Margaret Street to Victoria Tower. (This is the tower at the other end of the building from Big Ben.)

3. WESTMINSTER ABBEY

Westminster Abbey is important as the scene of coronations of English sovereigns and as the burial place of many famous and not so famous English people. But the best reason to see the Abbey is to experience it as an architectural treasure. Some people think that it is the finest example of the early English Gothic style in England (except for Henry VII Chapel, which is equally splendid but in the Perpendicular style).

Enter by the west entrance (where the bookshop is located). The nave roof was cleaned in 1965, and one should admire its "pristine splendor." The screen and the choir are mid-nineteenth century but impressive nevertheless. Proceed to the Chapel of Edward the Confessor. Next, go to the Henry VII Chapel—note especially the breathtaking fan-vaulting of the roof. Visits to the Poets' Corner and the Chapter House will complete your visit. The *Michelin Green Guide* gives as much detail as you are able to use in a short visit; but you might prepare beforehand by reading pages 11–19 of *Discovering London for Children*. Very detailed descriptions of the monuments and memorials inside the Abbey are given by the *Blue Guide* and the *Penguin Guide*.

Warning: Westminster Abbey is very crowded during the tourist season. Along with St. Paul's Cathedral and the Tower of London, it is one of the most popular places of interest in London. And crowds detract markedly from the Abbey's splendor. Our advice is to go at 9:30 A.M. or at 3:30 P.M.; these times give you a better chance to avoid the crush and still see the Royal Chapels and the Chapter House.

4. THE CHANGING OF THE GUARD AT BUCKINGHAM PALACE

DON'T GO! The crowds are huge, and it is difficult to see anything. To have a chance of seeing something, you have to get there early, at least by 10 A.M. And so you wind up spending a whole precious morning of your time in London peering over the heads of others at soldiers who appear to be motionless most of the time. You have more rewarding things to do with your time.

But if you must go, here are a few tips to increase your chances of enjoying it. The ceremony begins at 11 A.M. and consists of Guards Regiments and their bands marching to and from the Forecourt of the Palace; in the Forecourt the Old Guard hands responsibility over to the New Guard. So there are two kinds of things to see: first, the marching outside the Forecourt, and then the symbolic handing over inside the Forecourt. And there are good positions for seeing each of these, but unfortunately the best position for seeing one is not the best position for seeing the other. To see the marching only, station yourself at the extreme western end of the Mall, just on the side of the Victoria Memorial away from the Palace. Or, if you get there early enough, you can stand on the stairs of the Memorial—get as high up as you can, but don't sit on the statuary, because the police will just chase you off. Of course, in this position you are fairly distant from the Forecourt and the handing over of responsibility, which is also separated from you by a high iron fence. To see the handing over, you must arrive very early too and station yourself right against the fence, as close to the Main Gate as possible.

If you must go, it is a good idea to prepare yourself by reading a guide book called *The Changing of the Guard* (Lutterworth Press). This booklet is available at the Westminster Abbey bookshop and it is absolutely essential if you are to understand what you are (we hope) seeing. The booklet explains the insignia and history of the Guards Regiments, gives a step-by-step, diagramed account of the handing over, and also tells about other ceremonies that take place at St. James's Palace, the Tower of London, and Windsor Castle. It also describes the Queen's Life Guards and the Blues and Royals, which mount guard at the Horse Guards archway in Whitehall most mornings at 11 A.M. and which may also be seen marching down the Mall beforehand.

Although Green Park and Victoria tube stations are close by Buckingham Palace, we recommend that you go to Trafalgar Square instead and then walk through Admiralty Arch and down the Mall (not to be confused with Pall Mall, which runs parallel to the Mall). The Mall is a wide street bordered on the south by St. James's Park (which many think the finest park in London) and on the north by Carlton House Terrace and then by royal residences such as Clarence House and Lancaster House. This is a beautiful walk and may make your morning worthwhile, even if you don't enjoy the ceremony itself.

The Changing of the Guard is not performed every day. Before going, check by calling 730-0791, or 930-4466, extension 2356.

5. THE TOWER OF LONDON

The Tower of London is a large fortress, begun in 1077 by William the Conqueror and added to by his successors. It has been a residence of monarchs, a prison housing many famous people, and the repository of the Crown Jewels. The Tower contains a number of different towers, and several of these are essential sights for visitors. There is always a crowd at the Tower and usually long queues at several points within, but don't let this deter you. NEVER GO ON SUNDAYS. Before going, read *Discovering London for Children*, pages 27–37.

To get there, you can take an excursion boat from Charing Cross Pier (Embankment tube) or Westminster Pier (Westminster tube), and we recommend this method. Or you can take the tube to Tower Hill station, which is literally just across the street from the Tower. (If you go by tube after 10 A.M., you may be able to save money by buying a Cheap Day Return.)

Once there, buy your tickets on the west side of the Tower. Before you enter through the Middle Tower, stop at the bookshop on your right and buy a copy of the booklet *The Crown Jewels* (the official guide published by the government). You should also consider buying a copy of *The Tower of London* (also published by the government) for its centerfold aerial photo and its fine fold-out map in the back; but this is not absolutely necessary because the *Michelin Green Guide* provides a good map and an adequate guide.

Now, go directly to the Jewel House and begin your long wait in line, meanwhile reading the booklet on the Crown Jewels that you have bought, so that, once inside, you will know what you are seeing. The booklet on the Crown Jewels is not absolutely necessary either, because there are charts on the wall while you wait in line which describe the Jewels; but we feel that the booklet does a much better job, with a fuller description and color photographs. And the booklet and the charts together should make you an informed and appreciative visitor.

After the Jewel House, go directly to the White Tower. There is usually a line here too, though not nearly as long as at the Jewel House. The first floor of this Norman keep is devoted to displays of weapons. The second floor is St. John's Chapel, a radiantly beautiful Norman church in its original condition. This chapel is one of the finest parts of the Tower of London, and the visitor should pause long enough to experience its peace and dignity. On the third floor is an exhibition of armor. Throughout, the White Tower allows you to absorb the atmosphere of a medieval castle right in the heart of London.

Go next to the Bloody Tower to see Sir Walter Raleigh's quarters while he was a prisoner, and walk along the rampart (called "Raleigh's Walk") from which he would greet his admirers outside the wall.

Finally, go to the Beauchamp Tower (pronounced "Beecham") on the west side of Tower Green and inspect the inscriptions carved on the walls by prisoners. This is where the government guide *The Tower of London* comes into its own, since it tells the stories of some of the most interesting of these inscriptions. However, the Yeoman Warder on duty in this tower has a book that also tells about these carvings, and he will tell you about them if you ask him.

6. THE NATIONAL GALLERY

The National Gallery is one of the finest art museums in the world. It is also very large, and this makes it necessary for the visitor to decide how best to see what he or she wants to see. The Gallery distributes a small brochure that lists fifteen of its most important paintings for the visitor who can spend only an hour or two there. We suggest that you make several short visits rather than try to see everything at one time. Many people find that they have seen in an hour or two as much as they can absorb anyway. And at least several times during your visit you will doubtless be in or near Trafalgar Square where the Gallery is located.

The main part of the collection that is on exhibit can be surveyed in a reasonably unhurried way in three visits of about two hours apiece, one visit devoted to the Italian rooms, a second for the Dutch and Flemish paintings, and a third for the French, British, and Spanish. The *Michelin Green Guide* is very helpful here; it shows these parts of the Gallery in different colors on a floor plan with each room numbered and keyed to a brief catalog of contents. *Let's Go: Britain and Ireland,* pages 76–78, has brief, helpful appreciations of some of the more important masterpieces.

7. THE VICTORIA AND ALBERT MUSEUM

The V and A, as it is usually called, shows all of the exuberance and inexhaustibility of the Victorian temperament, of which it is a product. There is room after room of furniture, glass, ceramics, tapestries and carpets, stained-glass windows, metalwork, jewelry, and much more. There is no way to see the V and A quickly. The visitor's best strategy is to decide which type of work he or she wants to see most and then concentrate on that. Here again the *Michelin Green Guide* is of great help with its color-coded and numbered floor plans.

Remember that the V and A is closed on Fridays and open only from 2:30 to 5:30 P.M. on Sundays. The nearest tube station is South Kensington where an underground passage will take you right into the museum.

8. ST. PAUL'S CATHEDRAL

St. Paul's must be seen, however little time you have in London. Try to visit it soon after visiting Westminster Abbey, to compare two very different ways of expressing religious wonder and devotion. St. Paul's took thirty-five years to build, after the Great Fire of 1666 destroyed Old St. Paul's—a very different style of church—and is Sir Christopher Wren's masterpiece.

Enter under the twin towers at the west. There are monuments in the church (and the *Blue Guide* and the *Penguin Guide* give good accounts of these), but we suggest that you spend most of your time experiencing the splendor of the architecture achieved by the rhythm of arches of increasing height as one walks up the nave, until this rhythm is crowned by the soaring dome at the transept. Guide books will give you all the figures on the size of this church, but as with Westminster Abbey, all of these facts fade into insignificance beside the experience itself. First, walk around in the nave and in the north and south aisles and then sit quietly for a time in the nave.

You should also enter the Crypt (by a stairway on the eastern side of the south transept) to view the tombs of Wellington and Nelson, and particularly the funeral carriage (said to be made from the metal of captured guns) that bore Wellington's body. Even now, this somber, craggy machine expresses the sorrow that England felt at losing him.

Before leaving, stop at the bookstall inside the church and buy a copy of the guide booklet *The City of London Churches* (published by Pitkin; also available in some London bookshops). This booklet gives excellent brief descriptions of other churches in the City along with many excellent photographs of both interiors and towers; and it will help you to decide which other City churches to visit.

Getting to St. Paul's is easy. Simply take the tube to St.

Paul's Station, which is directly north of the church a little distance away.

Major Places of Interest on the Outskirts of London

9. HAMPTON COURT

The visitor should devote at least half a day to Hampton Court Palace and the grounds. Even if you have little interest in royalty, the Hampton Court experience is still very rich and exciting. The Palace itself is partly in pure Tudor style and partly in Wren's classical style and is a joy to look at. Inside you will find a marvelous collection of paintings—by Bruegel, Giorgione, Tintoretto, and others—which belong to the Queen and which are worth the trip by themselves. The drawing rooms, galleries, and halls are sumptuously decorated and atmospheric. Outside the Palace are some of the most beautiful gardens in England, long vistas over lakes, and a fine walk along the Thames.

There are several ways of getting to Hampton Court. One can go by excursion boat from Westminster Pier; but we do *not* recommend it. The boat stops at many places along the way and the trip takes four hours one-way; so you would find yourself spending most of your time on the river and not have enough time to see Hampton Court itself. The fastest way to get there is by suburban rail train from Waterloo Station; the train stops at Hampton Court Station. Another fairly fast way is by Green Line Bus numbers 716, 716A, or 718. One can also take a combination of tube and bus—by tube to Wimbledon and then bus 131 through Raynes Park and Kingston to let you off right outside the Lion Gates. (Be sure to take a 131 that goes as far as Hampton Court; you catch the bus right across the street from the tube station.)

You will need to buy the official guide when you get there. The *Michelin Green Guide* assumes that you have it, the *Blue*

Guide is too brief, and the *Penguin Guide* has nothing at all on Hampton Court.

If you enter by the Lion Gates, first go through the Maze, which is close by (you will get lost for a few minutes there). Then proceed to the West Front, through Base Court, and to the southeast corner of Clock Court where you will find the entrance to the State Apartments. Your tour of the State Apartments will end with the Great Hall (note the hammer-beam roof) and you will exit into Base Court. Go out to the West Front and turn left down to the Thames. Turn left again and walk along the Barge Walk on the waterfront, entering the grounds again through a gate after a few hundred yards. Ramble back through the grounds, finally coming to the walk that runs along the east front of the Palace. Before you get to the Palace itself, turn left along the south side of the Palace, and enjoy the Pond Garden, the Privy Garden, and the Great Vine. (If you are there at the end of August or the beginning of September, you may buy Black Hamburg grapes from the Great Vine.) Finish your visit with a stroll along the Long Water (extending east from the east side of the Palace).

10. GREENWICH

Greenwich is another garden of delights, although of a rather different sort: sailing ships, Wren architecture, the first classical villa in England, a fine naval museum, and the Old Royal Observatory. Time has a way of passing quickly at Greenwich, so plan to spend the better part of a day here.

If the day is warm enough, take the excursion boat from Charing Cross Pier or Westminster Pier. In this way you will get a guided tour of the most interesting part of the Thames riverfront: St. Katharine's Dock, the pub "The Prospect of Whitby," Execution Dock, Rotherhithe, Deptford. Other methods of getting to Greenwich are: tube to New Cross and then bus 177 or 53; directly from Central London by bus 188; or by rail from Charing Cross or Waterloo Station to Maze Hill Station.

First, go through the *Cutty Sark* and Francis Chichester's *Gypsy Moth IV* at the riverfront. Then walk up King William Walk (directly from the stern of the *Cutty Sark*), and at West Gate, just before the Dreadnought Seaman's Hospital, turn left past the hospital and into the Painted Hall of the Royal Naval College. This is one of the most impressive rooms in England. Also see the Chapel in the mirror-image building across the quadrangle. Then resume walking in your former direction and cross Romney Road to the Queen's House and the National Maritime Museum. The Queen's House helped to introduce Palladian, or classical, style to England. Compare the Queen's House with the Royal Naval College to see how the original classical style was developed and extended by Wren.

Finally, stroll through Greenwich Park behind the Queen's House and go up the steep hill to the Observatory. Be sure to go inside Flamsteed House to see the Octagon Room with its elegant paneling and color scheme; this is one of those rooms in which one could live forever because of its perfect beauty. Also, everyone will want to straddle the prime meridian with one foot in the Eastern Hemisphere and the other foot in the Western.

If you take the boat, be sure to check when the last return trip leaves the pier so that you will not be left high and dry.

11. KEW GARDENS

These are the Royal Botanic Gardens and primarily aim at the identification of plants and the dissemination of botanical information. But for the general public, the Gardens are pure pleasure and exhibit amazing variety.

Getting to Kew Gardens is extremely simple: take the tube

to Kew Gardens Station (District line, but be sure to take a train on the Richmond branch, not to Wimbledon or Ealing Broadway); you will find yourself in the main square of the little town of Kew with two long streets forking in front of you; take the left-hand street (Lichfield Road), and after five minutes' walk you will be at Victoria Gate on the east side of the Gardens. Admission is one pence! At this point the fullpage map of the Gardens in the *Michelin Green Guide* will prove invaluable.

Here is our advice on how best to see the Gardens. Go first to the iron and glass Palm House very near the Victoria Gate. Notice the Queen's Beasts in front, particularly the Red Dragon of Wales, the Lion of England, and the Unicorn of Scotland. Walking around the Pond in front of the Palm House, you will encounter the vital Chinese Guardian Lions, probably sculpted in the eighteenth century. Heading northward, notice the Temple of Aeolus, one of the many garden follies whose only purpose is to surprise and delight. Walk through the Aquatic Garden (north of the Alpine House) and then go westerly to the Orangery (one of Sir William Chambers' masterpieces) where you may visit exhibitions and buy books and postcards. But don't linger at the Orangery. Move immediately west to Kew Palace, the only remaining former royal residence in the Gardens. This house is on a much smaller, more intimate scale than Hampton Court or Windsor. The King's Breakfast Room has fine paneling. Notice the ceiling and wallpaper in the Queen's Boudoir, the elegant color schemes (with matching draperies) of the Queen's Drawing Room and the King's Bedchamber. The formal garden behind the Palace indicates the medicinal purposes of some seventeenth-century plants. After a stop at the refreshment stand nearby, walk to the river and stroll along River Side Avenue until on your left you see the Lake. At this point you will also see Syon House across the Thames with its lion at the very top. Now walk in toward the Lake and into the pine groves, and you will soon encounter a long vista (the Cedar Vista) through the pines ending at the Pagoda. This is the most imposing walk in the Gardens. Along the way, on your right, examine the carving on the Japanese Gateway. Going back to the Victoria Gate from the Pagoda, you will pass other charming garden follies, including the Ruined Arch and King William's Temple.

Spring and summer are, of course, the seasons when Kew is at its most glorious, but the landscaping, vistas, buildings, and follies can be enjoyed in any season.

12. WINDSOR CASTLE

Windsor Castle offers great rewards for anyone interested in architecture, military fortification, painting, history, or royalty. St. George's Chapel alone makes the visit worthwhile for the Perpendicular Gothic perfection of its nave and fan-vaulting, its resplendent choir and chancel, and its twin oriel windows. Well-preserved fifteenth-century timbered buildings fill the Lower Ward. The State Apartments have, for the most part, a quite different feeling to them from that of the State Apartments at Hampton Court—grander but perhaps more remote and austere, though at the same time very ornate. The Waterloo Chamber and St. George's Hall are especially impressive. And the paintings hung in these apartments can occupy one's attention for hours by themselves.

Near the State Apartments are two exhibitions. The first is Queen Mary's Doll House, delightful for persons of all ages, with its associated collection of dolls from all over the world. The second is the Exhibition of Old Master Drawings, including works by Leonardo, Raphael, and Michelangelo; to our minds the most exquisite drawings are those of Thomas More and his family by Holbein. We especially urge you to spend a bit of time at this exhibition. Reproductions of these works are on sale here.

To get to Windsor Castle, take the tube to Paddington and then the British Rail train from Paddington Rail Station. Be sure to change trains at Slough (pronounced to rhyme with "sow" and "plow") or you will find yourself in Reading or Oxford in no time at all. The first sight from the train of the Castle rising from the midst of the town of Windsor is thrilling.

The *Michelin Green Guide* gives no guide at all to Windsor, nor does the *Penguin Guide;* the *Blue Guide* has only a relatively short section on it. We suggest that after entering the Castle through the King Henry VIII Gateway, you go to the bookshop on your left and buy the *Walk-Round Guide to the Precincts of Windsor Castle* by Sir Robin Mackworth-Young (published by Pitkin). This is a superb point-to-point tour that is keyed to a very readable map. Inside St. George's Chapel, purchase (for 2p) the small brochure called *St. George's Chapel,* which gives a point-to-point tour of the interior of the Chapel. *The Official Guide to Windsor Castle* describes the State Apartments and their furnishings in great detail.

Part Four

LESS FREQUENTED PLACES OF EXCEPTIONAL INTEREST

The major places of interest dealt with in the preceding section should (with the exception of the Changing of the Guard) be visited by everyone if at all possible. And since many, many people do visit them, they are often quite crowded. In this section, we have picked out some exceptionally interesting places that are visited by only a small fraction of visitors to London. Some of them are totally unknown to the average London visitor and even to London residents. These are places for those who want to delve more deeply into the treasures of London, for those who hate crowds or wish to get off the beaten track, for those interested in London's history, and for those who simply love beauty. Many of these places can be seen in an hour or less and can be taken in as part of a walk in the area or on a special short trip directly to the place of interest itself. We have grouped these places together by neighborhood or geographical area, beginning with the area around Trafalgar Square. And we have given complete directions on how to get to each place.

Whitehall
1. THE BANQUETING HOUSE

Whitehall is the street that runs from Trafalgar Square to the Houses of Parliament. Since it is lined with buildings housing branches of Her Majesty's Government, such as the Foreign Office, the Treasury, and the Ministry of Defense, the word "Whitehall" has come to be synonymous with the executive branch of the government while the word "Westminster" is used to refer to the legislative branch. Most visitors go to Whitehall to see Number 10 Downing Street, the residence of the prime minister. However, this is a mistake. Number 10 Downing Street is the greatest single disappointment to visitors in London because there is literally nothing special there to see—just an ordinary town house façade ornamented by two policemen. Skip Number 10 Downing Street, and go instead to the other side of Whitehall at the corner of Horseguards Avenue (directly opposite Horse Guards Archway with its mounted guard on duty).

Here stands the Banqueting House, built in 1619 by Inigo Jones at the command of James I, and another (with the Queen's House at Greenwich) of those buildings that inspired the classical style of the eighteenth century. The Banqueting Hall inside lies at the top of a stone staircase and is one of the most beautiful rooms in Central London. It is another room that one could live in forever because of its perfect proportions, its ceiling paintings by Rubens, its elegant color scheme and windows. As in the Painted Hall at Greenwich, a rolling cart covered by a mirror enables one to examine the ceiling paintings without endangering one's neck.

It is not unusual to be the only one in the Hall while outside Whitehall teems with tourists.

Trafalgar Square

2. ST. MARTIN'S-IN-THE-FIELDS

As you stand at Nelson's Column in Trafalgar Square facing the National Gallery (north side of the Square), the Church of St. Martin's-in-the-Fields is at two o'clock, facing on St. Martin's Lane at the corner of Duncannon Street. It will have a familiar appearance to Americans because many American churches have the same combination of a classical façade and a spire, but there was and is much controversy about this combination in England. However, it is the interior that will excite your admiration. The Corinthian columns, the gilding, the arches and galleries, the elliptical ceiling, make this one of the handsomest churches in Central London. On one of your passages through the Square, spend a few minutes here.

3. THE NATIONAL PORTRAIT GALLERY

If you know anything at all about English history and culture, you owe it to yourself to spend a couple of hours in the National Portrait Gallery. It is part of the same building as the National Gallery and is entered from the west side of St. Martin's Place, near the confluence of Charing Cross Road, St. Martin's Lane, and William IV Street.

The collection is of portraits of well-known English men and women, arranged chronologically. To begin at the beginning, take the lift to the top floor. Free brochures are available in many rooms giving the historical context of the individuals portrayed, and these are supplemented by charts and explanations posted on the walls. This is one of the most pleasant ways to learn or brush up on your English history. But, as with the National Gallery, you will need to come back several times to see the whole collection. There is too much to take in on just one visit.

St. James's
4. LANCASTER HOUSE

Lancaster House is outfitted like a small palace and is perhaps the grandest house in London. It contains a famous double staircase decorated with marble of varied colors and set off by a background of fluted Corinthian columns. Other attractions are Italian Baroque ceiling paintings, beautiful French clocks and mirrors, and seventeenth-century paintings. Chopin played here for Queen Victoria.

Locate the House by walking down either the Mall or Pall Mall away from Trafalgar Square and turning at Stable Yard Road. Coming from Pall Mall, the House will be on your right, and coming from the Mall, it will be on your left. It is open only on Saturdays and Sundays from March until late autumn, 2 P.M. until 6 P.M.

5. THE QUEEN'S GALLERY AND THE ROYAL MEWS

Buckingham Palace, the Queen's London residence, is not open to the public. (Nor is the nearby St. James's Palace, the official residence of monarchs from William III until the accession of Queen Victoria in 1837.) However, the public is welcome to visit a chapel, rebuilt after air-raid damage, on the south side of Buckingham Palace. This is the Queen's Gallery, which contains changing exhibits of fine art from the extensive royal collection (some of which may also be seen at Hampton Court and Windsor). We suggest combining a visit to the Queen's Gallery with a visit to the nearby Royal Mews, which houses the royal coaches, horses, and parade harness. (A mews was originally a row of stables and coach houses, with living quarters above.)

But to combine these visits, you must plan carefully because the Royal Mews is open *only* on Wednesdays and

Thursdays from 2 to 4 P.M. On a Wednesday or Thursday, try to get to the Queen's Gallery (which opens at 11 A.M.) soon after lunch. This will allow you an hour or two at the Gallery, with plenty of time to visit the Royal Mews before it closes at 4 P.M.

To get there, take the tube to Victoria Station. Coming from the station, turn right and walk about 500 yards north along Buckingham Palace Road. The Royal Mews is on your left at the corner of Lower Grosvenor Place, while the Queen's Gallery is about 100 yards up the road, again on your left.

6. ST. JAMES'S PARK AT NIGHT

Many Londoners consider this the most beautiful park in London, though Regent's Park has many champions too. At noon during the week, civil servants and members of Parliament relax here, along with businessmen and women, particularly at the Duck Island end of the lake.

We strongly recommend that on a nice evening you walk down the Mall to Marlborough Road and turn left into the park. Continue on this path until you are standing on the bridge over the lake. On your right is a vista leading to Buckingham Palace, while on your left is one of the most romantic scenes in England, rivaling the famous view of the lake and the Grand Bridge at Blenheim. The fountain near Duck Island is lit up and has the lighted façades of buildings in Whitehall as a backdrop. In such a setting you might expect to meet Ingrid Bergman and Charles Boyer strolling together.

7. PICKERING PLACE

In every part of Central London, there are small courts and streets behind the buildings that line the main streets. St. James's has several of these, and one of the best is Pickering

Place. But you will have to be alert to find it. Go down St. James's Street from Piccadilly. Before you reach Pall Mall, you will find Berry Bros. and Rudd, Wine Merchants, at Number 3 St. James's Street. On the north side of this building (that is, the side closest to Piccadilly) you will find a narrow paneled passageway. This is Pickering Place; and at the other end of the passageway, you will find a quiet, dignified court with lovely Georgian-style buildings. It is an oasis of serenity hidden away in the middle of Central London.

8. QUEEN ANNE'S GATE

Queen Anne's Gate is not, strictly speaking, in St. James's. But it can be easily found by walking through St. James's Park, over the bridge, and then out of the park and across Birdcage Walk. Queen Anne's Gate is the street directly opposite this exit from the Park.

This street contains the best Queen Anne domestic architecture in London. Notice especially the canopies over the doorways and the elegant windows with their brick trim. One or two of the houses on the north side of the street have the original black ironwork torch snuffers and boot scrapers, and you can imagine yourself being lighted by torch to a dinner party at one of these houses. (Other torch snuffers can be seen on the east side of Wimpole Street between Devonshire and Weymouth streets; and there is an especially magnificent set at Number 68 Gloucester Place, near the corner of Dorset Street.)

Pimlico

9. THE TATE GALLERY

There are two important collections here: British painting and modern art. The British wing is dominated by Turner, whose amazing development from conventional landscapes, ruins, and towns through classical Roman scenes to those splendid blazes of light and color is clearly and fully laid out for you here. The Turners alone are worth the trip. One special feature, easily missed, is the Pre-Raphaelite Room (Number 28), reached by going downstairs from Room 14; works by Rossetti, Holman Hunt, and Millais give you an opportunity to see if there really was any unity to the Pre-Raphaelite Brotherhood. The modern collection is good, with Picasso, Giacometti, Max Ernst, and others.

The nearest tube is Pimlico and the way to get to the Gallery is clearly marked from the station by signs. If you get lost anyway, just go down to the river and then walk north. Unfortunately, there is little else to see in the vicinity of the Tate.

Kensington

10. KENSINGTON PALACE

The State Apartments at Kensington Palace are well worth seeing. Their chief glories are the ceilings of the Privy Chamber and of the Cupola Room, the latter being set off by Ionic columns and pilasters and by statuary arranged in apses. Queen Victoria was christened in the Cupola Room, with her names being decided upon through discussion as the Archbishop of Canterbury held her over the font. The long galleries are impressively proportioned. And be sure to see the garden behind the Palace.

We think that the best way to approach Kensington Palace is through Kensington Gardens, the large park east of the Palace. Get off the tube at Queensway and go directly across the street and into the park; now, walk down the Broad Walk right in front of you, and the Palace will be on your right about halfway down the Walk.

The Strand
11. THE YORK WATER GATE

Take the tube to Embankment Station and walk out of the station on the city side rather than on the Thames side. Cross the street diagonally into Victoria Embankment Gardens, bear to your left through the band-shell seating area, and in about fifty yards you will be at the York Water Gate. This gate was the entrance from the Thames to York House, owned by George Villiers, Duke of Buckingham (every one of whose names has survived in the street names of the area—there was even an "Of Alley"). If you were going to dine at the duke's house, you might pull up to this gate in your barge and then go the short remaining distance on foot. Charles I probably dined here with Buckingham, his political ally with the House of Commons.

The main reason to see the Water Gate is to appreciate the enormous energy and confidence of the Victorian engineers and, by reflection, of the Victorian Age itself. This Water Gate stood at the edge of the Thames from 1626 until the late 1860s when the Embankment was built and the Thames pushed back. Not satisfied with altering the Thames, the Victorians built bridges over it, which are still in use, and even changed the course of other London rivers. The Serpentine in Hyde Park is the Westbourne River dammed up and part of it put underground by the Victorians. If you happen to be in the Sloane Square tube station, look overhead and you will see a giant square iron conduit fifteen feet above the platform and the track. This pipe carries the Westbourne after it leaves Hyde Park and is the original pipe installed a century ago. These remarkable engineering feats were all typical of an age that considered nothing to be impossible.

12. THE HUNGERFORD ARCHES

After seeing the Water Gate, go through the Gate, turn left along the pavement (do not go up the stairs behind the Gate) and you will come to Villiers Street. Turn right along Villiers Street until you are about halfway between the Embankment Gardens and the Strand, and look to your left. You will see a dark, arched passage under the Charing Cross Rail Station. This is called the Hungerford Arches. A walk through the Arches to Craven Street is one of the most sinister experiences in London. The Arches are historically important through being at the general location of a shoe-blacking factory where Charles Dickens at age twelve was put to work. It was a traumatic experience for him and greatly influenced his later work. This experience is also the source of David Copperfield's term of service in Murdstone and Grinby's bottling warehouse (which Dickens set in Blackfriars rather than here).

Covent Garden

13. ST. PAUL'S, COVENT GARDEN

The Covent Garden market is now closed and awaiting redevelopment (with the market itself situated at Nine Elms on the South Bank), but don't let this stop you from visiting the area. From the Covent Garden tube station, go to your right down James Street, crossing Floral Street, and continue down James to Covent Garden, the square containing the abandoned market. Turn right and then turn left at the very next cross street. This brings you in front of St. Paul's, Covent Garden, and its impressive east portico featuring a beautiful pair of lamps. Although this portico appears to be the main entrance to the church, in fact the main entrance is at the other end. It is said that when the designer conceived of the east portico, he forgot that the altar was to be placed in the eastern end too, forcing the main entrance to the other end of the church.

This church is memorable as the scene of the opening of George Bernard Shaw's *Pygmalion,* from which the musical *My Fair Lady* was derived. If you have seen the film made from Shaw's play, you will remember the marvelous scene in which, in a great downpour of rain, Eliza Doolittle, the Covent Garden flower seller, first encounters Henry Higgins, and in which Higgins correctly infers Colonel Pickering's background merely from his accent.

14. GOODWIN'S COURT

This can be approached from St. Paul's, Covent Garden, by going back up to King Street and turning left, following along while King Street becomes New Row and then turning left again at Bedfordbury. Or you can come from the Leicester Square tube up Cranbourn Street to St. Martin's Lane, turn right to New Row, turn left along New Row and then right at the next intersection onto Bedfordbury. In either case, once you are coming down Bedfordbury, you must keep a sharp lookout along the west side of the street, because Goodwin's Court is a little alley that runs between Bedfordbury and St. Martin's Lane. It is completely charming and has the best eighteenth-century bow windows in London. If you look very carefully, you may be able to spot figures of animals above some of the doors. It is said that these were symbols of the companies that insured these houses against fire and that each had its own fire-fighting outfit before the days of the municipal fire departments; the symbol told which company of fire-fighters to call in case of fire.

Marylebone—Regent's Park
15. HOME HOUSE

This jewel of a house is almost unknown to London visitors and to Londoners as well. It is the finest remaining example of a Robert Adam town house. Built for a wealthy Jamaican widow, it features a great circular hall that rises up the entire height of the house and contains a staircase of surpassing elegance that divides into two sections halfway up. Each room is beautifully designed, and the ceiling decorations and apsidal niches are particularly interesting. The whole interior is a fully successful solution to the problem of providing a light, colorful, cheerful environment as a retreat from a cloudy, wet climate.

Home (pronounced "Hume") House is at 20 Portman Square. It belongs to the Courtauld Institute of Art of the University of London whose main gallery is located at the university in Bloomsbury. Guided tours (free) of Home House are available. Call first to find out when the House is open to visitors (usually every weekday when the university is on vacation and on Saturdays when the university is in session) and to be sure that a guide will be there when you arrive. (Look up the number in the phone directory under "Courtauld Institute, 20 Portman Square.") Take the tube to Marble Arch, then go left down Oxford Street to Portman Street, turn left and go past the Churchill Hotel, turning right immediately on the north side of the Square. Number 20 should now be in front of you, several houses from the northwest corner of the Square.

A fine book by Dr. Margaret Whinney describing the House in detail is available inside the House for about £1. It contains not only photographs of the House but also drawings by Robert Adam from the large collection of architectural drawings in the Sir John Soane Museum. These drawings alone are worth the price of the book.

16. THE WALLACE COLLECTION

The Wallace Collection is fairly well known, but we mention it here to make sure that you know about it too. Though well known, it is not awash with huge throngs of people, and this doubles the pleasure of a visit to it. It is a human-sized art museum with many masterpieces and excellent collections of French furniture and porcelain. Reminder: the museum offers free gallery tours on Wednesdays at 1 P.M. and on Fridays at 2:30 P.M.; this is the best way to begin an acquaintance with the Collection.

To get there, take the tube to Marble Arch. Emerging from the station, turn left to go along Oxford Street; just past Selfridges Department Store, turn left on Duke Street and go on up Duke Street to Manchester Square. The Wallace Collection stands on the opposite side of the Square.

17. FITZROY SQUARE

This is one of London's most attractive Georgian residential squares, with distinguished terrace housing on all four sides. The Square was laid out by Robert Adam, and the houses on the east and south sides were built by him in 1790–94. A plaque on Number 29 (on the west side) states that Virginia Woolf, the novelist, and George Bernard Shaw lived here in the late nineteenth and early twentieth centuries. The houses in Fitzroy Square should be compared with those in Bedford Square (see below), Harley Street and Wimpole Street, and the north side of Portman Square, among other places, for an overview of Georgian town-house architecture.

Take the tube to Warren Street. Turn left from the station

and walk west on the Euston Road to Fitzroy Street, turn left and walk fifty yards down to the Square. A visit to Fitzroy Square could easily be combined with a visit to Regent's Park.

Bloomsbury
18. BEDFORD SQUARE

This is another Georgian residential square with houses even more attractive and elegant than those in Fitzroy Square. The doorways of these houses repay close examination. Notice the stone castings around the doorways, with faces in carved relief at the top (for example, at Number 36). The fan lights over the doors are especially handsome. Notice also the moldings and reveals (areas between window frames and outer walls) painted in light colors and the ironwork balconies.

Bedford Square is right across Bloomsbury Street from the British Museum and can easily be seen before or after one of your visits to the Museum. The nearest tube station is Tottenham Court Road. Walk up Tottenham Court Road away from Oxford Street, past the intersection with Great Russell Street to Bedford Avenue. Turn right and go past Morwell Street to Adeline Place where you turn left into the Square.

19. CHARLES DICKENS'S HOUSE

Dickens and his family lived here for three years, and the house is now a Dickens museum well worth seeing. Moreover, a visit to this house allows you to examine the interior and layout of a late-eighteenth-century Georgian house. Typically tall and narrow, often with five or six floors, the Georgian house nevertheless gives the impression of spaciousness, partly through the use of tall windows. This could be a valuable model to use in attacking the housing problems of our time.

At this house you can see the china monkey which Dickens always had standing on his desk and without which he could not settle down to work, a blacking pot of the type Dickens worked with as a boy of twelve at the Hungerford Stairs (see comments on the Hungerford Arches above), furniture, manuscripts and letters, and other interesting mementos. The Dickens House is also the headquarters of the worldwide Dickens Fellowship.

Take the tube to Russell Square Station and then walk on Guilford Street away from Russell Square past the Great Ormond Street Hospital and Coram's Fields. Doughty Street is on your right just before you get to Gray's Inn Road. Now turn right and find Number 48 on the east side of Doughty Street.

Unfortunately, there is not much else to see in the immediate neighborhood of Doughty Street. But perhaps lovers of literature will also be encouraged to visit this area because of another, though less imposing, literary association with Doughty Street. Harriet Vane, in Dorothy Sayers's *Strong Poison*, is said to live at 100 Doughty Street while on trial for the murder of her lover, Philip Boyes; Lord Peter Wimsey succeeds in proving her innocent, proposes marriage, and is finally accepted in what is, to our minds, Sayers's best novel, *Gaudy Night*.

20. THE PERCIVAL DAVID COLLECTION

This collection of Chinese pottery is an absolute gem, very quiet and relatively little visited. Every piece is exceptional and is superbly exhibited. The Victoria and Albert Museum contains more Chinese pottery (as it contains more of just about everything), but the Percival David Collection is the place for learning and appreciating. The Collection contains examples of all the important styles, from Tang celadons and northern and southern Sung stoneware to Ming porcelain and Famille verte and Famille rose. Buy the illustrated guide by Margaret Medley, which gives you exactly what you need to know on a point-to-point tour.

Get off the tube at Russell Square and take Bernard Street one block to Woburn Place. Turn right up Woburn Place to Tavistock Place, and then go left for two blocks to 53 Gordon Square (which is at the very southeast corner of the Square). Ring the bell for admittance. *Warning:* Call before you go to make sure that it will be open when you arrive (387-3909). The Collection sometimes is unexpectedly closed; and if you don't call first, you may find yourself turned away at the door.

21. THE COURTAULD INSTITUTE GALLERIES

This is another jewel of a museum on a human scale, with as much on exhibition as most people can take in on one visit. The Lee and Gambier-Parry Collections contain early Italian paintings, Old Master paintings, ivory, majolica, and Islamic objets d'art. The Courtauld Collection is one of the finest French Impressionist collections anywhere. This museum is usually uncrowded and a quiet delight.

From the Russell Square tube station, go down Bernard Street across Woburn Place and then across the north side of Russell Square. Take the first right after the square and then (at Woburn Square) another left and a right to bring you to the middle of the west side of Woburn Square which the Galleries face.

Holborn

22. SIR JOHN SOANE'S MUSEUM

Although this museum is small, it is so packed with interesting objects that you may not be able to see it in one visit. There are marble carvings, bronze statuettes, reliefs, Hogarth's famous series *A Rake's Progress,* ruined cloisters, fine furniture, medieval woodwork, columns complete with capitals, capitals without columns, the sarcophagus of Seti I, portions of friezes, fifty-three volumes of drawings by the Adam brothers, and much more. The place is a treasure trove and will fascinate you because its seemingly random arrangement produces new surprises around every corner. The ideal time to go is on Saturdays when, at 2:30 P.M., a public lecture tour is given. On the last Saturday of each month, a special treat is provided when the tour is led by the Museum's director who, in recent years, has been Sir John Summerson, the distinguished historian of architecture. There are no hordes of tourists here and your visit will be very pleasant.

From the Holborn tube station, turn left to go south on Kingsway, then turning left at the third street (Remnant Street). Go along Remnant Street to Lincoln's Inn Fields (a large square). The Museum is at Number 13 Lincoln's Inn Fields, which is near the middle of the north side of this square. It is closed on Sundays and Mondays.

Fleet Street

23. DR. SAMUEL JOHNSON'S HOUSE

Probably best known as the subject of Boswell's biography, Johnson was a man of letters and the author of a fine dictionary of the English language—fine, not in covering more words than earlier dictionaries, but in giving more precise definitions and in basing his work on the whole range of English literature. That dictionary was compiled in the garret on the top floor of this House, a beautifully proportioned room. Other rooms are filled with Johnson memorabilia, well exhibited with descriptions on handboards in each room. At the desk near the entrance, you may purchase an attractive reproduction of a map of Johnson's London (1731) in either black and white or sepia. The map shows that London's western boundary then was Hyde Park and that London barely extended north of what is now Oxford Street. We suggest that you buy a copy (for 50p) and take it home to enjoy in America.

Get off at Blackfriars tube station, walk away from the river on New Bridge Street to Ludgate Circus and then left (away from the blue railway bridge) down Fleet Street. As you pass the Daily Telegraph Building, you will see Hind Court on the north side of Fleet Street; this will take you to Gough Square and to Johnson's House at Number 17. When you leave the House, we suggest that you turn sharp right at the foot of the front stairs and follow Johnson's Court back out to Fleet Street.

24. PRINCE HENRY'S ROOM

This building is an early-seventeenth-century, timber-style house. It is not quite as old as Staple Inn on Holborn, but it overhangs the street in a similar manner and, unlike Staple Inn, one can go inside. The large room on the first floor (American second floor) has fine Tudor oak paneling on the west wall and Georgian pine paneling on the other walls. The ceiling is of intricately decorative plaster.

Go to the Temple tube station and then away from the river up Arundel Street to the Strand. Turn right, pass Temple Bar (the monument in the middle of the street with the City Griffin on top) and find Number 17 Fleet Street just by the west side of Inner Temple Lane.

The City

25. ST. BARTHOLOMEW THE GREAT

If you admired the limpid beauty of St. John's Chapel in the White Tower at the Tower of London, you should make a special effort to see St. Bartholomew the Great. The Norman Choir is original twelfth century (though the startling oriel window on the south side is sixteenth century). Even the approach to the church is fascinating—under an Elizabethan gateway and into a peaceful churchyard from which one can see Romanesque arches on the exterior wall.

Get off at Farringdon tube station. Emerging from the station, turn left and walk up Cowcross Street and across Charterhouse Street, passing through Smithfield Market. This brings you to Little Britain Street. Then go along Little Britain Street until you reach the timbered gateway.

26. THE MUSEUM OF LONDON

This is a new museum combining the collections of the Guildhall Museum and the old London Museum in Kensington Palace. Do not miss this if you are at all interested in history. The star of the show is the resplendent Lord Mayor's coach, but the museum contains all sorts of other fascinating things, such as cells from Newgate Prison (very creepy), old storefronts, Roman relics, medieval antiquities, clothing and stage costumes, and so on.

From St. Paul's tube station, cross Newgate Street (going away from St. Paul's Cathedral) and walk directly north up St. Martin's-le-Grand; at the roundabout intersection with London Wall (which is a street), climb the stairs to the raised concrete platform above the street. You enter the museum off this platform. While on this platform, look at the new highrises of the Barbican, a housing development intended to induce more people to live in the City (and at the tower of St. Giles Cripplegate lost among the new buildings). Farther along this platform, you can see a section of Roman wall in the garden of St. Alphage.

27. LEADENHALL MARKET

The right time to see Leadenhall Market is at the noon hour on a weekday. Then it is thronged with workers in the City and the Market lives! This is the place to come to buy the makings for dinner if your taste runs to pheasant, grouse, rabbit, and other delicacies, all of which are prominently displayed on the front counters. The late Victorian construction of the Market is characteristic of its times, but some would like to tear it down to allow excavation of the old Roman basilica thought to be underneath the Market.

Get off at Monument tube station, and walk up Gracechurch Street (the path of an old Roman street) and across Fenchurch. The Market is on the right-hand side of Gracechurch Street about halfway between Fenchurch and Leadenhall streets.

The South Bank

28. SOUTHWARK CATHEDRAL

Westminster Abbey, grand as it is, is not a cathedral because it is not the principal church of a diocese and it does not contain a bishop's throne. However, this honor does belong to Southwark Cathedral which the *Blue Guide* rightly calls "the finest Gothic building in London after Westminster Abbey." It also has a great advantage over Westminster Abbey, namely that it is uncrowded. Very few people visit it, and therefore it can be experienced as it was meant to be experienced. Try to visit this church at a time when an organ recital is being given, for which it is a perfect setting. The Jarrold guide, which can be purchased inside, gives an excellent point-to-point tour.

Getting to Southwark Cathedral is easy. Take the tube to London Bridge Station. The cathedral is directly across Borough High Street; you will see its tower with the four pinnacles rising above the street level. (Incidentally, "Southwark" is pronounced "Suth-ark.")

29. THE GEORGE INN

The George is the last galleried coaching inn left in London. As a coach passenger, you could drink your ale in one of the galleries while watching your coach being loaded in the courtyard below. Many have concluded that Dickens was referring to this inn when he wrote in *The Pickwick Papers:* "Great, rambling, queer old places they are, with galleries, and passages, and staircases, wide enough and antiquated enough to furnish materials for a hundred ghost stories. . . ." Have dinner or at least a half-pint here.

From London Bridge tube station, turn left and walk down Borough High Street. The inn is in the third alley on your left on the east side of the street after the intersection with St. Thomas Street.

Hampstead

30. KEATS HOUSE AND FENTON HOUSE

Fenton House was built at the very end of the seventeenth century, in the time of William and Mary, and is agreed by everyone to be the most beautiful house in Hampstead. Now owned by the National Trust, it contains fine English porcelain and an extensive collection of early keyboard instruments that will intrigue music lovers. Be sure to walk around the House to enjoy its exterior and its walled garden.

Keats House, built over a century later, was the residence of the poet John Keats during the last years of his life, and the interior of the House is similar to what it was during Keats's time. The sitting room has the original windows with their shutters and Keats's bookshelves. There is a museum in the Chester Room with manuscripts, letters, relics, books, and portraits. Americans will be proud to learn that this house was saved from destruction in 1920–21 by contributions largely from the United States. The setting of the House is lovely, at the edge of Hampstead Heath, and an appropriate place for the composition of some of his finest poetry.

Take the tube to Hampstead Station (the deepest station in London). Walk up the High Street (literally "up" since Hampstead is on a slope), passing Heath Street on your right. Upon reaching the street called Hampstead Grove, turn right. Fenton House is a little way up on your left. Then come back down the High Street, past the tube station, to Downshire Hill, turn left and then, a little farther on, turn oblique right onto Keats Grove. Keats House is identified by a plaque over the door and lies on the right side of the street. Retrace your steps to the tube station, or try this alternate route back which will give you a view of the Heath (a very large park) itself: On leaving Keats House, turn right and continue down to South End Road, which runs along the Heath. Turn left and continue up along the Heath (the road becoming East Heath Road) until you reach Well Walk. Turn onto Well Walk and, at the intersection with Willow Road, bear slightly right along Flask Walk, which brings you right to the tube station.

31. KENWOOD HOUSE

This is a stately home close to Central London and mainly the work of Robert Adam. The east wing is the Adam Library, with its warm colors dominated by rose and blue. There is a fine dome in the hallway and a chastely beautiful staircase. The Iveagh Art Collection is hung here, including two of the greatest portraits in the world, *Pieter van den Broecke* (also called *The Man with the Cane*) by Frans Hals (compare with Hals's *Laughing Cavalier* in the Wallace Collection) and Rembrandt's *Self-Portrait in Old Age,* a painting full of wisdom and experience.

Kenwood is at the northern edge of Hampstead Heath and a rather long but pleasant walk from the Hampstead tube station. If you decide to walk, follow the excellent map on page 90 of the *Michelin Green Guide,* which indicates the trails through the Heath very clearly. Start from Well Walk in Hampstead and turn left before you get to Parliament Hill and its famous view of the London skyline.

Hounslow
32. OSTERLEY HOUSE AND PARK

Located in a five-hundred-acre park containing dense woods and beautiful lakes, Osterley House is a dazzling triumph in interior decoration by Robert Adam. He designed everything, including the furniture and the rugs, and much of it is still in place. The effect is (to use his own words) "all delicacy, gaiety, grace, and beauty." The Great Portico at the front is said to have been inspired by the Temple of the Sun at the ancient Syrian city of Palmyra, while the Etruscan Room shows the influence of Pompeii. The library here should be compared to the very different Adam Library at Kenwood. The paintings over the bookcases are by the remarkable Angelica Kauffmann. She was a founding member of the Royal Academy and later a friend of Goethe in Rome during his Italian journey. The country atmosphere at Osterley provides a pleasant relief from the city, and the House gives an experience of refinement and elegance not to be missed.

Osterley House is much easier to get to than Kenwood, being directly on the tube (Piccadilly line; stop at Osterley). The *Michelin Green Guide* contains a helpful room-by-room tour as well as a history of the House. Open for only four hours in the afternoons (closed Mondays).

Hertfordshire

33. HATFIELD HOUSE

Hatfield House is about twenty miles outside of London. But it is such a pleasure and so easy to reach from Central London that we want to recommend it specially to you.

The House is a Jacobean country home built around 1608 by Robert Cecil, the chief minister of James I. It still belongs to the Cecils—the excellent guide to the house was written by the contemporary man of letters, Lord David Cecil—and has many associations with English political history. One member of the family who lived in this house, the third Marquess of Salisbury, was prime minister three times between 1855 and 1902.

Hatfield House is richly decorated, with extensive use of wood carving and paneling. The huge Marble Hall has as fine a minstrels' gallery as you will see anywhere. Each pillar of the Grand Staircase is surmounted by a beautifully carved figure. The Long Gallery, where ladies could take exercise in bad weather by walking up and down, is 180 feet long, running the entire length of the house. The Armory (a closed-in portico) has fine English tapestries. And the Library glows with fine book bindings. It is instructive to compare this house with others—such as Kensington Palace—from quite different periods. You are allowed to see the House only on a guided tour, which, fortunately, is excellently handled. On the grounds, you may also see the surviving Banqueting Hall of the Old Palace (1497), a good example of fifteenth-century architecture and once a residence of James I.

You can get to Hatfield Station, just across the road from

the House, by rail from King's Cross Station in about half an hour; trains run frequently. Or you can take a Green Line Bus 716 or 716A from Marble Arch and see a bit more of the northern London suburbs on your way. The bus trip takes about an hour and a half. The House is open from the end of March to the beginning of October. Check with the London Tourist Board (730-0791) for exact visiting times.

Part Five

TWENTY ORIGINAL WALKS

In this section we describe walks and tours based on various themes. Some of these combine walking with visits to places of interest described in Part Four. Several of the walks take one through areas of the city that are interesting even though they may have no special points of interest to visit.

1.   A ROMAN LONDON WALK

This walk will take you to several of the more accessible Roman survivals and at the same time give you a look at some features of the City.

Begin at Tower Hill tube station. (1) Turn right as you come out of the station and go up the street (Cooper's Row) a few yards to a courtyard (at 8–10 Cooper's Row) on the right side of the street. Go into this courtyard and all the way to the back. Here is a section of the old city wall which is Roman up to ground level (the Roman section has layers of red tile among the layers of stone) and medieval above ground level. A plaque on the south wall of the courtyard describes the site and its features. (2) Retrace your steps past the tube station and then turn left into Wakefield Gardens (between the station and the street), walking to the other side of the Gardens. Here is another section of Roman wall (again Roman below and medieval above) that you can walk right up to and touch, if you like. Here also, at the top of the stairs which lead down to the wall, is a cast of the restored tombstone of the Roman procurator, Julius Classicianus, a humane official who effectively protested the severe punishment of the Iceni rebels led by Queen Boudicca (Boadicea). (3) Now, go back up Cooper's Row to Pepys Street, turn left, and go down to Seething Lane. Turn right and find St. Olave's Church across the street at the corner of Seething Lane and Hart Street. Notice the tower with its lantern on top and its projecting clock. Samuel Pepys, the great diarist, and his family worshiped here; he and his wife are buried here, and there are busts of them in the church. Pepys lived for a time in Seething Lane. Notice the skulls above the churchyard gate. (4) Go down Seething Lane toward the river and across Byward Street to All-Hallows-by-the-Tower (also called All Hallows, Barking). From the tower of this church, Pepys watched the Great Fire of 1666 which destroyed most of the City. Inside is a Roman tessellated floor (in the crypt—ask the verger to see it), an excellent font cover, and brasses. (5) Leaving the church, continue for a short distance on Byward Street, curving down to Lower Thames Street. On the left side of the street are the Custom House and Billingsgate Fish Market. At St. Magnus the Martyr Church, turn right up Fish Street and pause to examine the Monument. (6) Then turn left and take Monument Street west to King William Street, turn right, and take King William Street a few yards up to Cannon Street, turn left and take Cannon Street about six hundred yards to Queen Street. Now turn right and then right again on Queen Victoria Street. A little way up the street is the reconstructed ground plan of the Temple of Mithras. Mithras was originally Persian, and Mithraism became Christianity's strongest rival, promising a happy life after death and emphasizing honesty, purity, and courage. (7) You can now continue up Queen Victoria Street to the great Bank intersection and inspect Mansion House, the Bank of England, and the Royal Exchange. There is a tube station at this intersection.

2. KENSINGTON GARDENS AND THE MUSEUMS

Go to Queensway tube station. (1) Walk almost directly across the street (the Bayswater Road) to the Black Lion Gate entrance to Kensington Gardens. You are now on the Broad Walk which gives one of London's widest vistas. (2) Halfway down the Broad Walk, turn right into the Kensington Palace grounds and tour the Palace. (3) Coming back out to the Broad Walk, turn right and go down to Kensington Gore Road. Turn left and eventually you will pass the Albert Memorial on your left and the round Royal Albert Hall (the home of the Proms concerts) across the street on your right. (Next to the Albert Hall is the Royal Geographical Society.) (4) Turn right at Exhibition Road and walk down to the Cromwell Road. At this point you can turn right for the Natural History Museum, turn left for the Victoria and Albert Museum (remember: closed on Fridays), or go back up Exhibition Road a little way for the Science and Geological museums. (At this intersection, there is also an entrance to the South Kensington tube station, which gives onto a tunnel leading to the station itself.)

3. SOUTHWARK AND LONDON BRIDGE

The walk combines a bit of sightseeing with a short walk across the Thames. (1) Go to London Bridge tube station. Then walk directly across the street (Borough High Street) from the station and enjoy a visit in Southwark Cathedral, a very fine Gothic church. (2) Emerging from the Cathedral, cross the street back to the tube station entrance and then walk down Borough High Street away from the river, past St. Thomas Street, and turn in at the third alley on your left (George Inn Yard) to visit the George Inn, the last galleried coaching inn in London (and now owned by the National Trust). (3) Walk back toward the river. As you reach London Bridge, you will see the statue of the Griffin, the emblem of the City of London, showing that you are now entering the City. This London Bridge was completed in 1972, replacing a bridge reerected in Arizona. The medieval London Bridge that one sees in old prints had houses and shops built along both sides. (One of these prints may be seen on pages 2 and 3 of the Pitkin guide *The City of London Churches*.) (4) As you cross the bridge, Tower Bridge and the Tower of London are on your right, while the black, twin-towered building on the north bank to your left is the Cannon Street Rail Station. Beyond the Cannon Street Railway Bridge lies the Southwark Bridge. Here you have an excellent view of the City waterfront. (5) Continuing directly on from the bridge onto King William Street will bring you shortly to the Monument tube station.

4. BLOOMSBURY SQUARES AND MUSEUMS

This takes in some interesting parts of the University of London campus in Bloomsbury. It involves very little walking.

(1) From Russell Square tube station, go west on Bernard Street to Woburn Place, turn right up Woburn Place to Tavistock Place and then left for two blocks to 53 Gordon Square, which is right on the corner as you approach the square. This is the Percival David Collection of Chinese ceramics. (Warning: Call before you start out to make sure that it will be open

when you arrive—387-3909.) (2) Emerging from the Percival David Collection, enter Gordon Square itself. The Square has a fence around it, but you should easily find an open gate; it is a public square. Gordon Square is one of the most pleasant squares in London, heavily wooded, with well-kept flower gardens and shrubbery, and you will enjoy a walk around it. (3) Emerging at the southwest corner of the square, notice the University Church of Christ the King and see the interior; next to it is a building housing Dr. Williams's Library of theology, also worth looking into. (4) Just south of Gordon Square is Woburn Square. Cross the street and walk a little way down the west side of Woburn Square. You will arrive immediately at the Courtauld Institute Galleries, a superb art museum emphasizing French Impressionists. (5) From the Courtauld, go back up to Gordon Square, turn left and go past the Victorian Gothic building of Dillon's University Bookstore and out to Gower Street. Turn left again and go three blocks down Gower Street to Bedford Square, a perfectly preserved Georgian residential square with fascinating architectural details. (6) Turn right to go along the north side of Bedford Square out to Tottenham Court Road, turn left and go down to Oxford Street where you will find the Tottenham Court Road tube station.

5. ST. PAUL'S CATHEDRAL AND THE MUSEUM OF LONDON

Get off the tube at St. Paul's Station. (1) The Cathedral is very close by, and you will want to spend an hour or so visiting it. (2) Emerging from the Cathedral, go back to the tube station and then across Newgate Street and up St. Martin's-le-Grand. At the circular intersection with the street called London Wall, climb the stairs to the raised concrete platform and enter the Museum of London from this platform. (3) On leaving the Museum, come back down the stairs from the raised platform and find Little Britain Street a few yards back down St. Martin's-le-Grand. Turn right into Little Britain Street and then turn right with this same street as it curves north. After about 350 yards, you will find the timbered gateway of St. Bartholomew the Great on your right. Go in and discover this fine old church with its superb Norman choir. (4) Then go back down Little Britain Street the same way you came (it becomes King Edward Street) all the way to Newgate Street. You will notice the tower of Christ Church, Newgate Street on your right at this intersection; the remainder of the church was destroyed during the Blitz in 1941. Here you can also see the remaining wall of an old Franciscan monastery which originally stood on this site. (5) St. Paul's tube station is now right across the street.

6. ACROSS THE THAMES FROM THE SOUTH BANK ARTS CENTRE

Take this walk for a splendid river view and a look at several of London's South Bank theaters.

(1) Take the tube to Waterloo Station. Inside the station, you must look for signs saying "The South Bank"; these will bring you out on York Road where you will see a raised walkway over the road. Climb the stairs and take this walkway. Soon you will see signs indicating the various theaters in the Centre. Explore this area. The National Theatre (which is the furthest of the buildings from the raised walkway) is open all day long and can be entered without purchasing theater tickets. There are several restaurants in the building, and art exhibits and small concerts often take place in the lobbies (free of charge). Walk out on the balconies and terraces to enjoy a magnificent panoramic view of London from Westminster to St. Paul's. (2) Then go along the riverside terrace in front of the Royal Festival Hall and climb the stairs to the Hungerford Foot Bridge, which runs along the east side

TWENTY ORIGINAL WALKS 85

of the railway bridge going to Charing Cross Rail Station. While walking to the North Bank on this foot bridge, you will be rewarded with another beautiful view, the Thames riverfront downriver. (3) At the other end of this bridge, you will find the Embankment tube station right across the street. But before getting on the tube, you may wish to explore the area near this station: the York Water Gate, the Hungerford Arches. And if you wish to do more walking, go on Tom Pocock's "Down the Strand" walk (page 21), which begins from this station (called "Charing Cross Station," its old name, in Pocock's text).

This walk is wonderful both in the daytime and at night. We urge you to take it at both times. London along the river at night presents one of the most stirring sights in England when viewed from the South Bank Arts Centre.

7. AROUND REGENT'S PARK

One of the most impressive walks in London is around the Outer Circle of Regent's Park, past Regency terraces now over one hundred and fifty years old but as beautiful as when they were new. You will be overwhelmed by their size, variety, and classical splendor. Very few people take this walk, but it is not to be missed. The walk is fairly long—about two and a half miles—but remember that you are always only a few steps away from Regent's Park where you can, if necessary, rest on benches and enjoy the Park too. If you take enough time and rest when necessary, this long walk turns out to be only a delightful stroll.

Follow the map on page 129 of the *Michelin Green Guide* and its text on pages 127–28. (1) Begin at the Baker Street tube station and walk west on Marylebone Road to Baker Street, turn right and go up to the Outer Circle. The first terrace (on the west side of the Outer Circle) will be Clarence Terrace (the third item from the bottom on page 127 of *Mi-*

chelin). You then begin walking in a clockwise direction on the Outer Circle. (2) After reaching Winfield House (the home of the U.S. ambassador), you can cut directly through the Park (on paths marked plainly on the *Michelin* map) to Gloucester Gate rather than continuing around the Park on the northern side. (3) Chester Terrace, on the east side of the Park, is in many ways the aesthetic climax of this walk; be sure to view its long façade through one of the great arches at either end. (4) Then walk down to Marylebone Road, turn right, and you will find Regent's Park tube station a few yards down the road on the south side of the street. (5) Before taking the tube, you might look at the curved terraces on Park Crescent just behind this tube station.

8. REGENT'S PARK TO THE MALL

This walk shows London at its most citified, most urban, and in some ways its most handsome.

(1) Begin at Regent's Park tube station, go in either direction to Park Crescent just behind (south of) the station, and then around Park Crescent to Portland Place, a very wide north-south street. (2) Now head south away from the Park on Portland Place, noting the fine mansard roofs and classical façades on many of the buildings. These buildings house mainly embassies and company and institutional offices. At Langham Place, Portland Place becomes Regent Street. This transition is marked by the unusual conical spire of All Souls, Langham Place. (3) Continue on Regent Street across Oxford Street (this intersection is Oxford Circus), past the quality department stores and shops. Here notice the way in which Regent Street begins to curve to your left into Piccadilly Circus, a handsome vista called the Quadrant. (4) Pick up Regent Street again at the other side of Piccadilly Circus. Lower Regent Street now takes you through Waterloo Place with, first, the memorial statues of the Crimean

War (one representing Florence Nightingale), then (on your right) the Athenaeum, a London club for literary and artistic figures at the southwest corner of Waterloo Place and Pall Mall (note the Athenaeum's classical frieze just below the roof), and finally the Duke of York's column directly ahead. (5) Go down the stairs on the other side of the column to the Mall. Carleton House Terrace, on either side of the stairs, is in pure Nash Regency style—the same style as the Regency terraces around Regent's Park, thus forming an architectural unity at either end of the long axis of Regent Street. (6) Turn left at the Mall and go through Admiralty Arch to Trafalgar Square, where the tube awaits.

This walk is almost two miles long. There are tube stations at Oxford Circus and Piccadilly Circus along the way, in case you want a shorter walk along this same route.

9. MAYFAIR

Most of Mayfair is not interesting, and Tom Pocock spends much of his Mayfair walk wondering what has gone wrong with the neighborhood. Not that it has gone to seed—far from it. It is still very posh, but it is dull. Grosvenor Square is the most uninteresting square in London. We suggest that you substitute the following walk for Pocock's. We think that ours better emphasizes the interesting features of the area.

(1) Begin at Green Park tube station, walk four blocks down Piccadilly west toward Hyde Park, and turn right at White Horse Street, which will take you to Shepherd Street and the Shepherd Market. (2) Then take one of the streets going north out of the Market (Trebeck Street or White Horse under the arch) and come out on Curzon Street. Turn left and locate Crewe House at Number 15 Curzon Street on the north side of the street, a Georgian town house built in 1735 and still quite handsome. (3) Turn right just beyond Crewe House at Chesterfield Street. Go up to Charles Street,

turning left and then enjoying the lovely curve as Charles Street takes you to the forecourt of the Red Lion, a seventeenth-century inn with barrel seats outside. (4) Continue past the inn on Waverton Street to South Street. You should now be facing St. George's Primary School across South Street. Just to the right of the school, as you face it, there is an entrance to the pleasant Mount Street Gardens, one of those secret but public gardens completely hidden away behind buildings on all sides. (5) After relaxing in the Gardens, come out the same way you went in and go back down Waverton Street to Hill Street, turn left, and continue to the justly famous Berkeley (pronounced "Barkly") Square. Turn right into the Square and notice Numbers 50 and 52 at the southwest corner, beautiful original Georgian houses. Continue around the Square and inspect the interesting buildings at the northeast corner. (6) At this corner, turn around 180 degrees, come down the east side of the Square, and continue straight ahead down Berkeley Street to Piccadilly (with the Ritz Hotel across the street), returning to the Green Park tube station.

10. ST. JAMES'S PARK, QUEEN ANNE'S GATE, AND BANQUETING HOUSE

This walk is a bit over one mile and takes in several of the loveliest sights in London.

Begin from the Green Park tube station. (1) Walk on Piccadilly along Green Park to the first park entrance on your left, turn in and walk through the Park down to the Mall, then away from Buckingham Palace on the Mall. Or, alternatively, from the tube station, go away from Green Park on Piccadilly a few yards and then turn right onto Queen's Walk, taking it down to the Mall. Halfway up the Mall, opposite Marlborough Road, turn right into St. James's Park, continuing on to the lake and there enjoying the view from the bridge. (The buildings on the horizon past Duck Island and the fountain are in Whitehall.) (2) Continue through the Park on this path, coming out on Birdcage Walk and crossing this directly opposite the path to the street called Queen Anne's Gate. Turn left with this street, and inspect the Queen Anne houses, their doorway canopies, their dark brick and elegant windows. The statue halfway down the street on the south side is of Queen Anne. (3) Continue on, curving slightly left into Old Queen Street, then a sharp left at Storey's Gate and almost immediately another sharp right onto Great George Street, which takes you through Parliament Square. Make the first left from Great George Street; you are now in Whitehall. Walk down Whitehall, resisting the temptation to turn in at Downing Street to see Number 10 (very disappointing, as there is nothing to see), and go to Horse Guards Arch to inspect the mounted Guard there. Now go through Horse Guards Arch and through the building behind it into the great space known as Horse Guards Parade (with St. James's Park just behind it). To your right (north) is the Admiralty building, still carrying its short-wave aerial which was in use not so very long ago. (4) Coming out on Whitehall again, go directly across the street to the classical building on the corner, Banqueting House, and go inside to the Hall with its exquisite proportions, colors, chandeliers, and ceilings by Rubens. (5) After tearing yourself away from Banqueting House, you can continue up Whitehall to Trafalgar Square and the tube station on the southeast side of the Square.

11. THE STRAND, ST. MARTIN'S LANE, AND COVENT GARDEN

Begin at Embankment tube station. (1) First, go out of the station on the river side and up onto the Hungerford Foot Bridge (on your right as you leave the station) to admire the glorious view downriver. (2) Now, go back through the tube station and into Victoria Embankment Gardens across the street. Going through the band-shell area, you will find the York Water Gate on the other side. (3) Go through the Water Gate, making a sharp left immediately to go to Villiers Street where, halfway up the street, you will find the Hungerford Arches on your left. Go through the Arches (very sinister) and, upon emerging, turn right into Craven Street, and go on up to the Strand. (4) Cross the Strand in a slightly oblique right direction to Duncannon Street, then a sharp left down Duncannon Street, bringing you to St. Martin's Lane. Now turn right and go into St. Martin's-in-the-Fields, the church on your right, to admire its fine interior. (5) Continue on up St. Martin's Lane (by bearing right to avoid Charing Cross Road) to New Row. Turn right and then right again to come out on Bedfordbury. Come down the right-hand side of Bedfordbury and keep a sharp lookout for the alley known as Goodwin's Court, its bow windows and its quiet charm. (6) After seeing Goodwin's Court, go back out to Bedfordbury and back up to New Row. Then turn right on New Row and continue straight ahead for King Street (which is what New Row becomes). Continuing along King Street, turn right as you enter the Covent Garden Market Square to see the east portico of St. Paul's Covent Garden. (7) Continue around the Square and take the exit on the other side (Russell Street). Then turn left at the first corner and you will be on Bow Street and about to pass the Royal Opera House with its most regal façade (and its equally distinguished, in fact glittering, interior). (8) At Long Acre Street, turn left and you will see the Covent Garden tube station a short way down the street.

12. LEGAL LONDON

The Inns of Court are London's law schools, arranged, like the colleges of Oxford and Cambridge, with a hall (for dining), a library, a chapel, rooms for residences and offices, and a garden for walking and meditation. The four Inns are some of the most charming and picturesque places in London and should not be missed, even if your time is short. Their serenity, amidst the crowds and traffic jams of Holborn and the Strand, is remarkable.

(1) From the Chancery Lane tube station, look immediately across the street (to the south side of Holborn) at Staple Inn, a former Inn of Chancery (rather than an Inn of Court) whose Elizabethan façade survives from the late sixteenth century. (2) Then go to your right one block west on Holborn (away from Gray's Inn Road) and turn right into Gray's Inn. The gardens here are the most beautiful of all the Inns of Court. (3) Coming out the same way you went in, turn right, go to Chancery Lane, turn left down Chancery Lane, and then take either the first or the second right into Lincoln's Inn. Use the *Michelin* map (page 99) to tour Lincoln's Inn, noting especially the New Hall and Library (Victorian though in Tudor style) and the Chapel. (4) Then come down through New Square (of Lincoln's Inn) and out onto Carey Street, bear right and across the street, and walk through the Royal Courts of Justice, a late Victorian building with an immense Perpendicular-style Great Hall. You may be able to find an empty courtroom to visit here. (5) Come out of the other end of the Great Hall onto the Strand. Then turn left and walk up the Strand a few yards, crossing to the other side of the street and making the first right turn into Middle Temple Lane. At this point, follow the map of the Temple in the lower left-hand corner of the fold-out map of the City in the front of the *Michelin Green Guide*. Be sure not to miss the Temple Church, with its round church built by the Knights Templar, the original owners of this area. (6) By going back up to the Strand and turning left, you will find the Aldwych tube station down the street.

The London Walks organization's "Legal and Illegal London" walk is especially good because the guide will explain interesting facets of the British legal system to you. Take our walk only if their walk is not given while you are in London. (Note: Their walk does not normally include Gray's Inn.)

13. A CITY CHURCH WALK

This walk will take you through some of the most interesting parts of the City, including several features that are rather difficult to find. During this walk, use the *Michelin* map of the City and its description of various City churches (pages 51–60). We also advise arming yourself with Pitkin's booklet *The City of London Churches,* which can be purchased at major bookstores and at St. Paul's Cathedral bookstall.

Coming out of Tower Hill tube station, turn left and then right to go along Tower Hill Street, follow Byward Street to (1) All-Hallows-by-the-Tower. (You can see where this church is by looking directly west from the tube station.) Then go directly across Byward Street and up Seething Lane to the corner of Hart Street where you will find (2) St. Olave, Hart Street. Turn left onto Hart Street, then take the first left (to go south on Mark Lane), the very next right (to go west on Great Tower Street), and make the second right turn (at Rood Lane) where stands (3) St. Margaret Pattens. Then come back down Rood Lane across Eastcheap, and continuing down to (4) St. Mary-at-Hill. Now come down this street (St. Mary-at-Hill Street) to Lower Thames Street, turn right, and in two blocks you will be in front of (5) St. Magnus Martyr on the left side of the street opposite Pudding Lane. Then coming up Fish Street (also across from St. Magnus), you will cross Eastcheap and then Fenchurch Street (you are now on Gracechurch Street, an old Roman lane). On Gracechurch Street, just before the intersection with Cornhill and Leadenhall Street, there will be a tiny alley, St. Peter's Alley, on the left side of the street. This alley leads to (6) St. Peter's Cornhill. Come around on St. Peter's Alley and out the other side, bringing you to Cornhill. Turn left and go down just a little way to St. Michael's Alley on your left, which brings you to (7) St. Michael's Cornhill. Go on into the churchyard, being sure to notice the Jamaica Wine Shop and the George and Vulture Tavern. (Here you may begin to notice metal "Heritage Walk" markers set into the pavement.) Come back out on Cornhill, turn left, and go to Birchin Lane; here turn left again, going down to Lombard Street (which housed Italian bankers in the Middle Ages), turn right, and at the intersection of Lombard Street and King William Street, you will find (8) St. Mary Woolnoth. Now go through this large intersection, keeping Mansion House (the Lord Mayor's residence) on your left, and turn left immediately at Walbrook (along the west side of Mansion House), going down to (9) St. Stephen Walbrook. (The name "Walbrook" comes from a long-vanished tributary of the Thames, along which Romans built their town houses.) Now, go directly across Walbrook Street to Bury Street and along it to Queen Victoria Street. Turn oblique left, going down Queen Victoria Street, across Queen Street, and then oblique right up Watling Street to (10) St. Mary Aldermary. Continue along Watling Street to Bow Lane, turn right, and go up to (11) St. Mary-le-Bow. Then you can go back down Bow Street (south toward the river) directly to Mansion House tube station.

We have not included descriptions of the churches here because the *Michelin Green Guide* and the Pitkin booklet do a fine job of this. But each of these churches is a jewel and together they form one of the most impressive groups to be found anywhere.

14. SQUARES OF THE WEST END

This is a long walk. But it has the virtue that many of these squares are open to the public (though not all of them are), so that one can sit down and rest awhile when necessary. These squares are not really the main point of the walk. Instead, this is just a pleasant way of walking around in and getting to know the West End.

Begin at Piccadilly Circus tube station. Walk down Lower Regent Street (going south), then turn right at Charles Street and go into (1) St. James's Square. Coming out the opposite side of St. James's Square, go along King Street to St. James's Street, turn right and go up to Piccadilly. Now turn left and then turn right up Berkeley Street on the other side of Piccadilly. Berkeley Street takes you to (2) Berkeley Square. Find Bruton Street in the middle of the side of the Square formed by Berkeley Street, and take Bruton Street to New Bond Street. Directly across New Bond Street, you will find Conduit Street; go along Conduit Street one block, and then turn oblique left onto St. George Street which you will take up to (3) Hanover Square. Coming out of Hanover Square on the opposite side, take Harewood Place to Oxford Street; then go directly across Oxford Street and straight ahead up Holles Street to (4) Cavendish Square. Leave Cavendish Square at the opposite side, turning left to follow Wigmore Street about five hundred yards to Duke Street on your right. Turn right and take Duke Street up to (5) Manchester Square. (The Wallace Collection is here on the north side of Manchester Square, and you may wish to take a break by viewing the collection.) After a turn around Manchester Square, retrace your steps down Duke Street back to Wigmore Street and turn right, continuing on Wigmore Street across Baker Street to (6) Portman Square. (Home House is here, at Number 20 Portman Square, on the north side.) Then turn left to go down to Oxford Street, turn right, and find Marble Arch tube station a block down Oxford Street.

15. MARYLEBONE

Marylebone is a very pleasant and varied residential neighborhood lying between Regent's Park and Oxford Street. It gives one a concrete feeling for the idea that London is a city of villages because it retains some of its original village character—its High Street for example. (A high street is the shopping and business area of a town or village.)

(1) Begin at the Bond Street tube station and go oblique left across Oxford Street to James Street. James Street becomes first Thayer Street and then the Marylebone High Street, a lively, informal, and reasonably well-to-do street of shops. (Pronounce "Marylebone" as "Mar-le-bun," with the accent on the first syllable.) (2) At Hinde Street, turn right and continue down this street (which becomes Bentinck Street) to Welbeck Street. Turn left and at the very next corner turn right (onto Queen Anne Street), then go one block to Wimpole Street. Turn left and go up Wimpole Street. Elizabeth Barrett lived here when she met Robert Browning. They were married in the parish church of this neighborhood, St. Marylebone, at the upper end of the High Street. Notice the well-maintained Georgian terrace houses. These streets contain some of the best-preserved eighteenth- and nineteenth-century houses in London. (3) At Weymouth Street turn right. Here you have an excellent view of the universally excoriated Post Office Tower (which has a revolving restaurant at its widest point near the top). (4) Go half a block down Weymouth Street to Devonshire Mews South on the left-hand side of the street, and walk up the mews, one of the most delightful in this area with its pastel-colored houses. (5) Arriving at the far end of the mews on Devonshire Street, turn right and notice the Regency balcony on the white building at the corner of Devonshire and Harley streets. (6) Turn left up Harley Street to enjoy another beautiful Georgian block. (7) Walk up Harley Street to Marylebone

Road and turn left. At the second intersection turn left again, and you will be on the High Street at its northern end. St. Marylebone Church is on your right. Stroll down the High Street, eventually arriving at the Bond Street tube station again.

16. HANOVER SQUARE TO PICCADILLY

Here is a short walk that boasts no great sights but which explores an interesting area very briefly, the area between Regent Street and Bond Street. You can take this walk as part of a larger excursion to Piccadilly, St. James's, or Trafalgar Square.

Begin at the Oxford Circus tube station. (1) Turn left and walk west on Oxford Street just one block to Harewood Place. Turn left and go a very short way to Hanover Square. (2) Coming out of the opposite (south) side of the Square by way of St. George Street, go down to Conduit Street (noting on the way St. George's, Hanover Square, at the corner of Maddox Street, where Disraeli, George Eliot, Theodore Roosevelt, and Shelley were married). (3) Then make a sharp left, go one block, and turn right into Savile Row, the home of men's fine custom tailors. (4) At the south end of Savile Row, you will find the rear of Albany (flats for the wealthy), Burlington House (the Royal Academy of Arts), and the Burlington Arcade with its colorful banners and charming shop windows. (5) At this point you can either go through the Arcade to Piccadilly or else make a jog left into Sackville Street, which contains some interesting bookstores. (6) Arriving at Piccadilly, turn left for the tube at Piccadilly Circus.

17. BETWEEN PORTLAND PLACE AND BLOOMSBURY

This area has no special name and is not architecturally distinguished, but it has a vitality in its everyday life that is very attractive. Try to take this walk on a weekday noon.

(1) From Oxford Circus tube station, turn right to go east on Oxford Street for two blocks to Great Titchfield (on the north side of Oxford Street), turning left and going up to Mortimer Street. Turn right and stroll down Mortimer Street which soon becomes Goodge Street. (2) Just before you get to the main artery, Tottenham Court Road, you will cross Whitfield Street. If you turn left here, you will find Pollock's Toy Shop and Museum one block up Whitfield Street. The toy theaters should not be missed by anyone who likes the theater. (3) At Tottenham Court Road, turn right, and go down one block to Store Street. This is one of the most pleasant business streets in this part of London, with trees, little traffic, and a nice crescent at its west end (which is the mirror image of another crescent at the other end of Alfred Place on Chenies Street). Store Street brings you to Gower Street. (4) Turn right for the British Museum or go straight ahead for the University of London. (5) Or you can retrace your steps and then go left at Tottenham Court Road and down to Oxford Street for the Tottenham Court Road tube station.

18. SOHO

Soho is a seedy but lively neighborhood. It is a center of night life and contains London's Chinatown (on Gerrard Street), as well as some of its best Italian and Indian restaurants. Warning: there are many sex shops and pornographic movie houses here which advertise their wares openly; if this would offend you, skip Soho.

(1) From Oxford Circus tube station, take Argyll Street on the southeast corner of the Circus (right next to the tube station), noticing the fine house at Number 10 (left-hand side of the street) and the London Palladium, a famous variety theater. (2) At Great Marlborough Street, turn left and then take the first street on your right which will bring you into Carnaby Street, known for fashions for young people though

now past its prime. (3) At Beak Street, turn right and take the next left down to Golden Square and on down to Brewer Street, where you turn left. Go to Lexington Street and turn left, then up Lexington and right onto Broadwick Street. Three short blocks down Broadwick Street brings you to Berwick Street (pronounced "Barrack") with its widely known fruit and vegetable market. (4) The next street over (east) is Wardour Street, center of the British film industry, once booming and now struggling. (5) At Wardour and Broadwick streets, make a jog left and then right to go down St. Anne's Court, and then at Dean Street another jog left to take Carlisle Street to Soho Square, one of the most used and vital squares in the West End. (6) Turn left to go around Soho Square and take Soho Street from the north side of the Square to Oxford Street. Then turn right to the Tottenham Court Road tube station.

19. KNIGHTSBRIDGE AND SOUTH KENSINGTON

This is a rather posh area with a distinctive architectural style, very pleasant for a walk.

Begin at Knightsbridge tube station. (1) This is a good opportunity to see Harrods Department Store, and signs in the tube station will take you directly into the store. (2) Come out on the Brompton Road and turn left, just past Harrods, on Hans Road (named, like several streets in this area, after Sir Hans Sloane, whose collection formed the nucleus of the British Museum). (3) Then take the first right onto Walton Place leading to Walton Street. At Pont Street, turn left and then soon right again at Cadogan Square (pronounced "Cadug-an" with the second syllable accented). (4) Halfway down the Square, turn right onto Milner Street which leads to Denyer Street branching left. Turn right from Denyer Street onto Draycott Street and go on up to the Fulham Road.

(5) Turn left down the Fulham Road past Pelham Crescent and take the next right, bringing you to Onslow Square (which is quintessential South Kensington). (6) Continuing up this side of Onslow Square will bring you to the South Kensington tube station. (You are now very close to the South Kensington museums too.)

20. THREE WALKS FOR A NICE SUNDAY AFTERNOON

(1) Queen Mary's Gardens, Regent's Park

This is the most beautiful garden in Central London, with its small lake, the rock garden on an island in the lake, and the rose gardens. On a sunny Sunday afternoon, the garden is filled with English families relaxing. You can walk around the Inner Circle, along the Broad Walk, and on other paths. (Regent's Park tube station)

(2) The Victoria Embankment

Walk along the north bank of the river, beginning at Westminster tube station and ending at Blackfriars tube station. This is about one and one-quarter miles long.

(3) Hyde Park

Begin at Hyde Park Corner tube station. Enter the Park immediately, avoiding traffic-ridden and noisy Park Lane, and wander up toward Marble Arch. Near Marble Arch on Sundays, Speakers' Corner is usually in full swing, and you can listen to orations on almost any subject. Come out at Marble Arch tube station.

IMPORTANT PHONE NUMBERS

London Tourist Board (for general tourist inquiries): 730-0791
London Tourist Board daily recording of tourist attractions: 246-8014
London Transport (for travel questions): 222-1234
Weather: 246-8091
Information about children's events: 246-8007
Emergency: 999
Radio Taxis: 286-4848, 272-3030, 286-6010
In the U.S.: British Tourist Authority: 212-581-4700 (Address: 680 Fifth Avenue, New York, New York 10019, which is also the address of the British Travel Bookshop Ltd.)

Index

Adam, Robert, 65, 66, 75, 76
Albert Memorial, 81
All-Hallows-by-the-Tower, 80, 92
All Souls, Langham Place, 86
American Express, 8
Athenaeum, The, 87
Bank of England, 81
Banqueting House, 21, 38, 56, 89
Bedford Square, 22, 66, 67, 83
Berkeley Square, 88, 94
Bloomsbury, 12, 16, 37, 65, 67–69, 82–83
British Museum, 12, 32, 36, 39–40, 67, 97, 98
British Tourist Authority, 12, 13, 14, 101
British Travel Bookshop (New York), 31, 101
Buckingham Palace, 43, 44, 58, 59
Burlington Arcade, 96
Carlton House Terrace, 44, 87
Cavendish Square, 94
Changing of the Guard, 43–44
Chelsea, 29, 37
City churches, 90–96
City of London, 12, 16–17, 26, 28, 29, 72–73, 82
 Information Center, 33
City of London Churches, The, 48, 82, 92, 93
coin phones, 9
Courtauld Institute Galleries, 65, 69, 83
Covent Garden, 16, 27, 36, 63–64, 90
Crown Jewels, 45–46
Cutty Sark, 51
dentists, 11
Dickens, Charles, 63, 67–68, 74
East End, 17
Elgin Marbles, 40
English National Opera, 27
Fenton House, 74, 75

Fitzroy Square, 66–67
Fleet Street, 16, 38, 70–71
Gatwick Airport, 1
George and Vulture Tavern, 93
George Inn, The, 74, 82
Goodwin's Court, 64, 90
Gordon Square, 69, 82–83
Gray's Inn, 91, 92
Greenwich, 36, 50–51
Grosvenor Square, 87
guides, 31–32, 65, 66, 70
Hampstead, 38, 74–76
Hampton Court, 36, 41, 49–50, 52, 58
Hanover Square, 94–96
Harrods Department Store, 18, 33, 98
Hatfield House, 38, 77–78
Heathrow Airport, 1, 2
Henry VII Chapel, 21, 42
Home House, 65–66
Horse Guards, Whitehall, 44, 56, 89
Hungerford Arches, 63, 68, 85, 90
Hyde Park, 62, 71, 99
Jamaica Wine Shop, 93
Johnson, Dr. Samuel, house of, 22, 70–71
Keats House, 75
Kensington Gardens, 61, 81
Kensington Palace, 37, 61, 77, 81
Kenwood House, 38, 75–76
Kew Gardens, 37, 51–53
Kew Palace, 52
Lancaster House, 44, 58
Leadenhall Market, 73
Legal London, 90–92
Lincoln's Inn, 91
Lincoln's Inn Fields, 21, 70
London Bridge, 37, 82
London Tourist Board, 11, 14–15, 33, 42, 78, 101
London Transport Information, 4, 101

London Walks (guides), 24, 31–32, 37, 91–92
Magna Carta, 40
Mall, The, 43, 44, 58, 59, 87, 88
Manchester Square, 66, 94
Mansion House, 81, 93
Marylebone, 16, 37, 65–67, 95–96
Mayfair, 16, 87–88
medical care, 11
Mithras, Temple of, 80–81
money, English, 6–7
Monument, The, 80
Museum of London, 33, 38, 72–73, 83
National Gallery, 32, 36, 38, 46–47, 57
National Maritime Museum, 51
National Portrait Gallery, 37, 57
National Theater, 25, 84
Number 10 Downing Street, 56, 89
Old Royal Observatory, 50, 51
Open Air Theater, 26
Osterley House, 76–77
Painted Hall, Greenwich, 51, 56
Pall Mall, 8, 44, 58, 60, 87
Parliament, 17, 26, 36, 41–42, 56
Percival David Collection, 68–69, 82–83
Pickering Place, 37, 59
Pocock's *London Walks,* 28, 29, 36, 85
Pollock's Toy Museum, 97
Portman Square, 65, 66, 94
Prince Henry's Room, 21, 71
Queen Anne's Gate, 22, 38, 60, 89
Queen Mary's Gardens, 26, 99
Queen's Gallery, 58–59
Queen's House, Greenwich, 21, 51, 56
Regency Terraces, 85–86, 87
Regent's Park, 16, 22, 26, 38, 59, 67, 85–86, 95, 99
Roman London, 33, 73, 79–81
Rosetta Stone, 39
Royal Academy of Arts, 96
Royal Courts of Justice, 91
Royal Exchange, 81
Royal Festival Hall, 26, 84
Royal Mews, 58–59
Royal Naval College, 21, 51
Royal Opera House, 27, 90

St. Bartholomew the Great, 21, 38, 72, 84
St. George's Chapel, Windsor, 53, 54
St. James's, 16, 36, 37, 58–60, 96
St. James's Palace, 44, 58
St. James's Park, 38, 44, 59, 60, 88–89
St. James's Square, 94
St. John's Chapel, 21, 46, 72
St. Magnus Martyr, 80, 92
St. Martin's-in-the-Fields, 57, 90
St. Olave, Hart Street, 80, 92
St. Paul's Cathedral, 21, 26, 33, 43, 48–49, 72, 83, 84, 92
St. Paul's, Covent Garden, 63, 64, 90
Savile Row, 19, 96
Soane, Sir John, Museum, 66, 70
Soho, 16, 19, 38, 97–98
Soho Square, 98
South Kensington, 38, 47, 81, 99
Southwark Cathedral, 21, 73–74, 81–82
Speaker's Corner, 99
Staple Inn, 21, 71, 91
Strand, The, 16, 36, 62–63, 90, 91
Street Markets, 19
Tate Gallery, 37, 60–61
taxis, vii, 2, 4, 101
Temple, Inner and Middle, 91
Temple Church, The, 21
Ticket brokers, 25, 27–28
torch snuffers, 60
Tower of London, 17, 33, 36, 43, 44, 45–46, 72, 82
Trafalgar Square, 3, 27, 55, 56, 57, 58, 87, 89, 96
Victoria and Albert Museum, 37, 38, 47, 68–69, 81
Victoria Embankment, 62, 99
Wallace Collection, 32, 36, 66
West End, 12, 16, 17, 25, 94
Westminster, 17, 29, 56, 84
Westminster Abbey, 2, 17, 21, 36, 42–43, 44, 48, 73
Westminster Hall, 41, 42
Whitehall, 56, 89
Wigmore Hall, 26–27
Wimpole Street, 22, 60, 66, 95
Windsor Castle, 37, 44, 52, 53–54, 58
Wren, Sir Christopher, 48, 49, 50, 51
York Water Gate, 62, 85, 90
Young Vic Theater, 26, 27